'DOOG'

Also by Derek Dougan

ATTACK!
THE SASH HE NEVER WORE
THE FOOTBALLER
ON THE SPOT

'DOOG'

DEREK DOUGAN

READERS UNION
Group of Book Clubs
Newton Abbot 1980

To all young footballers who didn't make it.
After reading this book, maybe it's just as well.
And to all young hopefuls —
I hope they read it and find encouragement.

List of Illustrations

'Thanks for the Memory' Bill – and I'm not referring to Billy Bremner

No difficulty in guessing who scored

The King (Denis Law) and I

In days before advertising was fashionable on shirt fronts

The many faces of yours truly

Introduction

This is not a straightforward autobiography. It is an account of my experiences during the latter part of my playing career, including my early days in Northern Ireland playing for Distillery. I have dealt with my upbringing in Belfast in *The Sash He Never Wore*; and of my career at Portsmouth, Blackburn, Aston Villa, Peterborough, Leicester in *Attack!*.

If I move forwards and backwards in this book, taking sudden leaps in time, it is because no one's experience and any personal assessment are chronological. Events, incidents and impressions intermingle. New experiences re-shape previous judgments. Something happens and you are reminded of something else in the past. An active mind is forever reconsidering the past and trying to re-evaluate with hindsight. So it is in this book. If at times I am repetitive, it is because some glaring mistakes continue to be repeated in the game when by imaginative effort they could easily be overcome.

Things that happened to me at Wolverhampton Wanderers made me think again of my experiences at previous clubs and see them in different perspectives. I am not writing a history of events, but an impression of them from my viewpoint now that I am no longer a player but still bound to the game, emotionally and officially as the former chairman of the Professional Footballers' Association. I am trying to provide in this book a sum total of my experiences, mainly at Wolves, but also as a footballer aware of the game as a cut-throat business, which makes its participants, the players, suffer most.

It is the most insecure professional game in the world. Every year thousands of parents dote on sons they believe are destined to be the new Jimmy Greaves, Kevin Keegan, George Best, Pat Jennings, Trevor Francis, Bobby Charlton ... When their sons sign on the dotted lines, the way ahead appears to be a yellow brick road to football's Emerald City. Before they have reached

1

the age of twenty-two almost eighty per cent have dropped out of the game to find their living elsewhere.

Those who survive to stay the course soon find out that they have entered a world of insecurity, ruthlessness, competition and power-driving, in which the compensations are the thrills of the game and the adulation of the crowds. But of the chosen few, only a small proportion of them ever taste the true glory. Most are foredoomed to spend their playing careers in comparative obscurity with mediocre clubs, struggling to stay in business. There is no guarantee that once a player or a club reaches the top the position is impregnable. Fame and fortune can be transient.

All the clubs I joined were, or so I thought at the time, ambitious and anxious to explore and exploit the talent of the players on their books. It saddens me to see now what has become of Portsmouth, Blackburn Rovers, Aston Villa and Leicester City. Peterborough did not fulfil the promise of Gordon Clark's management, Aston Villa staged a revival but has not yet led the first division, and my last club, Wolves, is no way near to emulating the success of the fifties, the most momentous period in the club's 103-year history.

In the sixties I was asked to write about my footballing experiences, but I declined because I was not experienced enough. Now after thirteen years on the PFA committee and having become the association's longest serving playing chairman since the war, I have had time since I finished playing for the Wolves, five years ago, to assess my experiences.

If I appear to be bitter and cynical this is not my intention nor my true feeling. I am simply reflecting on my experiences and if, in some final analysis, they amount to a social study of a footballer's life and times, there may be lessons to learn. One lesson must certainly be that it is far better for managers to trust their players and regard them as allies than as threats to their own security, which was my own sad experience at Wolves.

I was proud – and still am – to be a Wolves player. Thrilled every time I put on the Wolves shirt, and proud when I ran on to the Molineux pitch that had been hallowed by Stan Cullis's team which in the fifties had humbled the footballing might of Europe.

The trophies packed in the display cabinets were for me not relics of the past but challenges. In seven years under the Bill McGarry regime, in this country all we managed to add were the League Cup and the Texaco Cup. It was a wretched environment, which I compare in this book to an open prison, at least as far as I was concerned. And yet my years with Wolves were the most satisfying of my career. This is no contradiction. I loved the club, but not the managerial dictates and the petty forms of discipline imposed on us, the players.

Why do I bother to go over those years with their irritations, frustrations and the petty squabbling? Why not let sleeping dogs lie? My answer is that I believe it is important, as well as interesting (I hope), for everyone who cares about football to know what players have to endure and what makes up their lives.

Most players spend their careers in awe of authority, knowing exactly who their masters are. Those who believe in making their voices heard because they have something constructive to give the game on and off the pitch, risk coming into conflict with managers, chairmen, directors and the football authorities who suspect their motives. Their lives can be made miserable if they are singled out as trouble-makers or rebels. At Wolves I was in the ironical situation of being at one with supporters, and at odds with the manager, at ease on the pitch and troubled away from it.

I searched my conscience to see if I had done anything to deserve the 'treatment' I was getting behind the scenes. I could find no rational explanation. I doubt if I ever will. My overwhelming obsession was the need to change the system, a system I felt operated against the true interests and the welfare of the players, the be-all and end-all of the game.

One

Voltaire is known in England as a French philosopher who is supposed to have said that though he disagreed with what someone said, he would defend to the death his right to say it. He probably didn't say it, but what he did say in Zadig made a lasting impression on me. 'A character in the story was vexed to find that fate had given him no share of the earth which equally belonged to all men.' I imparted the cause of my uneasiness to an old Arabian, who said to me: 'My son, do not despair; there was once a grain of sand that lamented it was no more than a neglected atom in the deserts; at the end of a few years it became a diamond and it is now the brightest ornament in the crown of the king of the Indies.'

At the start of my career as a footballer I was a grain of sand. I resolved to become not only a diamond, but the crown itself. Such is vaulting ambition which at times can overleap itself. In a career spanning a generation of twenty years, in England I tried to leap at the right moments. I made some errors of judgment and more than one or two mistakes. But after being known in the game as a 'rough diamond', the crowning glory came when I was elected Chairman of the Professional Footballers' Association, a particular irony that a player widely regarded as a rebellious individual, should be the leader of 2500 footballers, a point not lost on the sports writers when I was elected.

In the pages that follow I want to try to put together the atoms of my experience, as a player and as chairman of the players' union. Here and there I may appear to be splitting a few atoms and setting off explosive chain reactions. But that is not my intention. My purpose now that I am no longer a player is to describe what it was like, at the bottom and the top, and to reflect on the game which is the people's game, the greatest game in the world and one in which I still see my future taking shape.

One day you are out there looking for goals, the cheers of thousands ringing in your ears and you feel on top of the world. It's what life is all about, to a footballer. There's nothing else, nothing that really matters. That is how it feels on Saturday afternoons, the moment you emerge from the tunnel and see the coloured banners, scarves and a sprinkling of Union Jacks unfurl like a flock of brightly plumaged birds taking wing.

Then, one day, you are out there, away from the goals, looking for something else to do; something to take its place, knowing that whatever it is, it won't be the same. It can never be the same, because playing football, if you've dedicated your life to it, is the most satisfying form of self-expression imaginable. Imaginable, that is, to a footballer. Most players don't trust the specialist writers. Hunter Davies, who spent a year with Spurs and wrote about the club in a way they probably thought was going to be a public relations job, and which he made a warts-and-all close-up behind the scenes, knows from experience, or should know, how much they despise and dismiss all the outside experts.

They know the experts can write better and can even get a better perspective from the stands, but they also know that you've got to be inside the game, deep inside, to appreciate its meaning; what it means to a player who has put his heart and soul into something he knows will be wrenched from him within a few years.

I had the reputation, before I arrived at Wolves, as a perpetual wanderer, changing clubs every two years. I was able to take to Molineux an accumulation of experience which proved invaluable when I was elected chairman of the PFA. I knew from experience what it was like to be in the third division and I knew there was no real difference between divisions where problems, tensions and ambitions are concerned.

I regretted not picking up a championship medal en route. If two of my clubs, Blackburn and Leicester, had been aware of their players' skill and talent at crucial times, I might have had two. They were capable of winning the championship, but at administrative and managerial level appeared to be suffering from 'higher echelon' blindness which prevented these clubs seeing how easily they could have reached the top.

I found it curious at the time, when talent outstripped

6

ambition, why the sports writers did not latch on to it and ask why so much was being allowed to go to waste. They pride themselves on their perception and like to portray themselves as pundits, but neither at Blackburn nor at Leicester did any see that power was being deprived of glory.

It was ambition (or lack of ambition in other people) that made me move on. It was always ambition that kept me going, and if a club was not ambitious to fulfil its potential, I saw no reason to stay and waste my time, which would mean wasting my career.

Although it was a passing mood of futility and disenchantment at Villa that took me to Peterborough, I was glad of the third division experience. I used to say to Bobby Charlton, when he was a member of the PFA committee before he went to Preston as player-manager, that any player who has not played in the lower divisions, does not know what the game is really like.

In the first division most players are spoonfed. Everything off the pitch is done for them. On tour, all arrangements are made for them. Life at most of these clubs becomes a package deal. The danger is that by having so much done for them, first division players can sometimes become complacent and expect the best at all times. Not that it always was.

It has been encouraging, in recent years, to find some clubs forming co-operatives, enabling players to assume more active roles. I know of clubs where this idea is frowned on by managers who see them as threats to their own authority. In my view players should be encouraged to make the fullest possible use of their short time in the game and help their clubs on and off the pitch. Their experience could help managers to run more successful teams. There is a lot of prejudice to overcome, the most formidable being a common view among managers and boards of directors that footballers are 'as thick as two short planks' and should be kept in their places, on the pitch. Players being fined for writing articles, or giving their names to articles, in the press without club approval (which means vetting or censorship) is an example of how some feudalistic clubs treat their players as virtual prisoners, denied ordinary rights.

A footballer's career can be short. It can be a few years, eight

7

is the average if injury does not intervene. More could be made of players, on and off the pitch, if the system under which they operate were more flexible and sympathetic towards them.

I enjoyed eighteen years in the English League, more than twice the average span. Most players – about 80 per cent – do not last that long unless they slip into non-league football. We don't hear or read much about non-league football, until a side like Blyth Spartans gets within striking distance of the FA cup sixth round or a player like Jimmy Greaves is back in the news as a part-time player. And yet some good football is played by non-league clubs, as I discovered when I took over Kettering Town in the Southern League, which offered me greater administrative scope than the hidebound managerial system still operating at league clubs.

There is a lot of cut-and-thrust at non-league level and the dedication of fans, though fewer in number, is as passionate as you will find in the massed ranks at Anfield or Old Trafford. Kettering gave me deeper insights into the game than I imagined were possible after my long league experience, and I saw my arrival there as an extension of my career, not as a retraction.

At the beginning of my career, in my teens, I was ardently ambitious and determined to get to the top, as quickly as possible, and then to stay there. It had nothing to do with vanity, more to do with pride in the game and in myself as a player. If there is no pride, there is no dedication and ultimately no hope of survival.

In those far off days life and the game itself stretched out before me. The prospects were so far-reaching I was eager to wake in the mornings and get on with my life, which had to be based on football. Now, looking back, I see how life itself is intensified for a footballer, like the stage for an actor. But it is compressed into a few years. One moment, a footballer is a hopeful teenager and then, as though with one kick of the ball, he is a senior player and then reading about himself in the sports pages as 'a veteran'.

How did I stay the course so long? Dedication in training is partly the answer. Some players get bored with their clubs' training routines which can be monotonous and when this happens their days are numbered. They lose enthusiasm. My physique helped me to keep going and my style helped me to adapt to younger players just getting into their strides without losing my individuality. Long before I retired, sports writers were referring to me as Father Time, Mr Evergreen, the Irish Elder Statesman, culled from their pocketbooks of journalistic cliches reserved for any player who goes beyond the age of thirty. The descriptions were meaningless to me because I felt no differently playing for Wolves in my mid-thirties than I did when I was a raw recruit at Portsmouth.

Sometimes I contemplated going on until the fifty mark adding my name in the record books to Stanley Matthews and Billy Meredith. But those vintage stalwarts played in a different, less demanding age, when life for forwards was easier and much of the time they could wait downfield for passes from defenders. The notion of 'total football' was unknown.

A winger could take it easy, and often did, for stretches of a game and wait for the ball, then take off on a thrilling run down the wing. I used to hear at Leicester City, when I played there, how Charlie Adam, a left winger at Filbert Street in the late forties, would sometimes chat with spectators near the touchline and ask them the time, when he was waiting on the wing for the ball to be played to him!

These days a forward has to be a defender and a defender has to go forward. Positions are interchangeable, as managers call for non-stop running and talk about work-rate. The emphasis is on perpetual motion, which often disguises mediocre football and lack of ball control.

Extra demands are also made in training. In recent years training has become so intensive that I wonder if it is not being overdone. Time and again we hear of players being injured in training, pulling muscles, limping off with groin strains, damaged tendons and so on.

It's ironic, training is supposed to prepare players for Saturday matches and sometimes excessive training only rules them out of the matches. There were times at Wolves, after losing a mid-week game or giving a poor performance, when we would be called back the next day for special training when we did not have the heart or will for it. It would have been better for us to have had the day off to relax and get over the match.

If players are over-trained they can become stale and too exhausted by their weekday endeavours to be effective on match days. Boredom can set in from Monday to Friday, when the appetite for a competitive game should be whetted not dulled by routine. Forest are one of the few sides that realises this and give their players a couple of days off to recuperate.

Athletes are not driven nearly so hard. They space out their races whereas a footballer has to keep going, week after week, sometimes playing two, three or even four matches within seven days if fixtures pile up. The strain, which accumulates more in training than in actual matches, causes some top players to drop out of the game before their time. Injury takes its toll of such players as Denis Law. At Manchester United Bobby Charlton was reputed to have said that training bored him, by which I understood him to have meant that the routine was becoming a grind when United were going through a lean spell. Although I had a long playing career, I might have gone on even longer if I had eased up a little in training towards the end and not felt compelled to compete with younger players who were still developing their stamina.

I might have gone on, but to slow down if only a few yards in a race for the ball, would have lessened my effectiveness and that of the side. There is no sense in allowing a playing career to wind down and peter out in obscurity, for people to mutter: 'Look at him. You'd never think he used to be an international, poor devil.'

If there is anything more pathetic than a forgotten footballer it is a player trying to convince himself and the fans that he can still do it when his day has gone. He risks becoming a parody of his old self. I wonder, when I sometimes play in testimonial matches, whether it is wise for old favourites, once the idols of the crowds, to reappear with a middle-age spread and go through the motions again just to indulge a crowd's nostalgia. Those who remember their dazzling displays in the past see them now as pale shadows of their former selves or as bumblers. They can raise a cheer from their presence, but memories, I think, should be left intact and not overlaid by distorted images.

Having made the decision to retire at the end of my eighteenth season, I knew that my last game would be an anti-

10

climax. The boatman would be there, calling: 'Come in No. 10, your time is up.' Dramatising the situation, I felt it would be like being sucked into one of those astronomical black holes from which no energy or light can escape.

There were no real definite plans for the future. All I knew is that I could not and would not enter management, in spite of tempting offers, given the managerial hire-and-fire system. When the opportunity came to take over Kettering Town as chief executive, I did so because I had the freedom to try to develop the club along the lines I believe football clubs should be developed, as integral parts of sports complexes benefiting all sections of a community. The fact that it did not work out at Kettering as planned in no way invalidates the principle of bringing football clubs out of the mists of Victoriana into the progressive tail-end of the twentieth century. (I intend to enlarge on life at Kettering in another book, provisionally and perhaps, provocatively titled *How Not to Run a Football Club*.)

Soon to retire, I knew that the spotlights would dim and the cheers fade to a distant echo.

Consciously or subconsciously, footballers respond to cheers; they wallow in the adulation of the stands and terraces. They may sometimes get irritated by autograph hunters, but they know they would be more irritated if no one wanted their signatures. They like to see their pictures in the papers, their names in the sports columns, and the ball at their feet.

When all this is stripped away, as inevitably it must, life drops several degrees. The unknown stretches before you. For the first time, you are on your own. This is the crunch, the moment of truth when whatever remains of skill and talent has no market value.

The public are fickle. I don't say this accusingly. It's a fact of life. Heroes, stars and popular figures cannot expect to retain their popular reputation when they depart from the scene, unless they are exceptional like Henry Cooper and Bobby Charlton, who are granted the status of folk-heroes and continue to be welcomed wherever they go.

The paying public needs fresh faces and new heroes and it does not owe a player a living when he has finished playing.

And yet the public, in their innocence, fondly believe that all players are steering a course in their careers to ultimate

11

tax-havens, splendiferous night-clubs of which they are part-owners, to Majorcan beaches, world cruises, or estates in the country.

In the public mind is the thought that the ending of the maximum wage in the early sixties put footballers, en masse, in the super-tax bracket. The same delusion applies to motor-racing, golf and other sports. Jackie Stewart is seen not in isolation but as the personification of motor-racing. Tony Jacklin, who had a mansion in the Cotswolds and then went to the Jersey tax-haven, is seen to represent all British professional golfers, whereas Colin Snape, secretary of the Professional Golfers' Association, confirms that most of his 3000-odd members struggle to make ends meet. People read of the amount Billy Bremner got from his testimonial, they hear of the spin-offs that have come the way of Kevin Keegan, they know how much Bobby Moore paid for his new house, and they assume that all footballers are on to a good thing. Have you ever stood in a bar and heard the talk?

'They earn more in a year than I could make in a bloody lifetime.' 'Easy money, just for kicking a ball about.'

It is easy to forget the likes of Tommy Lawton, Wilf Mannion, Raich Carter, Hughie Gallagher, Pongo Waring, Dixie Dean and countless others who must have played the game for its own sake, because there was little monetary reward for them in their own day. They put their hearts and souls into the game and all they got out of it, in financial terms, was a pittance.

They were part of a system that was not challenged until the early sixties. I read with regret a few years ago that Wilf Mannion, once the golden boy of England's forward line, was working as a building site labourer. We have all been made painfully aware of Tommy Lawton's difficulties and his insecurity. When I read his autobiography, *When the Cheering Stopped* (Golden Eagle Press, 1973), I was almost moved to tears, of pity and rage, over the way he was treated by the game's administrators and legislators. Oh, the injustice and the pity of it all!

But let no one imagine that because the maximum wage was ended in the sixties, football has become a treasure trove for footballers throughout the league. Only a few enjoy fame and

12

fortune. Yet they all get the attention and the publicity, which persuades the public that all footballers are on easy street.

Most, particularly those in lower divisions, would be far better off, financially, working at a factory bench or in an office. I would be delighted, as the former chairman of the PFA, if all our members were earning a £100 a week basic wage today.

Nor should anyone imagine that there is so much security in the game today that talented players no longer fall by the wayside. I have seen some exceptionally talented players lost to the game, such as Danny Hegan and Jimmy Greaves. Jimmy's autobiography, *This One's On Me* (Arthur Barker Ltd, 1979), also saddened me in its description of his giving way to alcoholism and how this wrecked his career and his marriage.

The difference between then and now is that the PFA has a welfare and education officer, Bob Kerry, ready to advise and guide players to prepare for their future. It is tragic when some players fail to take advantage of the courses being offered to them and find themselves out of the game with no other livelihood. We don't usually hear of these sad cases, unless they involve former stars down on their luck. Stars, by definition, are people out of the ordinary, made conspicuous by the ordinary contributors around them.

For every player, in any sport, who reaches the top and enjoys the fruits of stardom, there are hundreds who play out their careers in the shadows. They might be just as dedicated, just as enthusiastic, but there is never much room at the top. Many are called, few are chosen.

George Best was called and chosen for super-stardom. He had his own place at the very top and then abandoned it, unable to match his temperament with the requirements of staying at the top and the responsibilities of power. He had what it takes on the pitch, but not off it and found two lives, as a footballer and as a showbiz personality, incompatible. His greatest failing, perhaps, is that he took himself too seriously when he was not playing and not seriously enough when he was playing. Or was it vice-versa?

A player might have plenty of skill and no charisma. Another may have a modicum of skill and plenty of charisma. The first might spend his career in relative obscurity while the other lives under a spotlight.

13

I have been lucky. Usually I have been in the right place at the right time, but it took a long while to find myself. Six clubs, in fact. Wolves might have signed me in the mid-fifties from Distillery. They looked me over through their scouting system and I knew they were interested, but nothing came of their inquiries. In those days, between 1953–7, I was centre-half and in later years I liked to kid Billy Wright that if I had been signed by Wolves I would have replaced him and altered the history of Wolverhampton Wanderers.

Instead I went to Portsmouth and began a journey to Molineux by a long circuitous route. The journey took ten years. My experience on the way taught me the value of finding the right club where I could feel at home. I was never completely at home at Portsmouth, Blackburn, Aston Villa, Peterborough and Leicester. Having said that and justifying every day I have spent with Wolves, I have to give Villa some qualification. Villa are a special club. Anyone who plays there enjoys a distinction which is rare in the game. Villa Park is 'hallowed ground'. It's a long time since they won the championship or FA cup, but Villa's traditions are undimmed. The past shines out of the players' boots. If any club has a divine right to prestige, it's Aston Villa. I am proud to have belonged to that select band of ex-pros who can say: 'I once played for the Villa.'

It's hard to explain the appeal of a club such as Villa. I have a feeling that it's not just the club itself, but the area in which it exists that provides the aura. Villa emerged when the Aston district of Birmingham knew poverty and hardship. There was a yearning there for excitement, drama and glamour. What better way was there to spend a Saturday afternoon after a hard five-and-a-half day week slog at the workbench – or trekking the streets looking for work – than to cheer Villa in the afternoon and Marie Lloyd or Dan Leno at the music halls in the evenings? The claret and blue were music hall colours, contrasting vividly with a drab environment. The history of Villa was etched in my mind when I arrived there and I craved to help make history, for Villa seemed to be on the point of a dramatic re-emergence.

If you have been with Villa you carry something special with you for the rest of your life. There are not many clubs

14

in that category, with the aura of glory long after the visible signs of it have receded into the past. Villa have not been a really great club for a long time, but the name conjures up images of greatness and echoes of glory. It was sad to find the start of the 1979–80 season marred by another power struggle in the boardroom after the departure of Andy Gray to Wolves. Struggles of this kind usually coincide with a team struggling to find form.

The Villa boardroom struggle reminded me of my own time at Villa Park, when I was given the boot in 1963. It is remarkable how a centre forward becomes a catalyst. What happened to me, happened sixteen years later to Andy Gray. A case of history repeating itself. The trouble is, they never learn!

When I arrived at Wolves, via Peterborough and Leicester, I sensed similar greatness, stemming from the momentous European days of the fifties, when the might of Europe fell at Molineux.

It is remarkable that this famous club, one of the twelve founder members of the league, should have had to wait until 1954 to win the first division championship for the first time.

The post-war years have been dominated in the league by Manchester United, Liverpool, Leeds, Arsenal and Tottenham, and recently, Nottingham Forest, though the front runners where championships are concerned, are Wolves, Manchester United and Liverpool. If Liverpool, well placed at the time of writing, go on to win the championship for the fifth time, they will be rightly acclaimed as the greatest club side of all time.

My eight year plus with Wolves saw only one major honour, the League Cup, which some fans still refuse to regard as anything more than the poor man's FA Cup. Even so, they were satisfying years, bringing my career to a climax and refuting those who said I was a wandering minstrel incapable of staying with one club for more than two years. I would like to have gone clutching a championship medal and FA Cup Winners' memento. But what I take with me has, perhaps, more enduring value – experience.

I have not only seen the game change over the years; I have experienced those changes, reacted to them and been forced to adapt to styles and systems unknown when I began playing in Northern Ireland. I have gone, according to my critics, from

15

rebel to committeeman, from Establishment knocker to Establishment negotiator. I don't know whether a police chief in the West Midlands was taking a tilt at me or trying to be colourful when he said my career was a classic example of a baddie turning goodie.

The truth is I have never been conscious of striking moral or amoral attitudes to justify myself in the game. I have taken what has come, tried to improvise and play it by ear when necessary, and apart from a little showmanship now and again, sought spontaneity in my style of play as well by conduct off the pitch.

It has been galling to be called a 'show off' or a 'trouble maker', but I can say that throughout my long career there is only one action for which I reproach myself. That is asking for a transfer from Blackburn Rovers on the eve of the club's FA Cup Final against Wolves. At the time I sought to justify it, saying that I was dissatisfied at Ewood Park and not to ask for a transfer, regardless of the circumstances, would have been dishonest. Looking back, it was an insensitive and indiscreet decision, which did more than anything else to brand me as an upstart and rebel. Anyone who could do that, said some of the commentators, could do anything; which wasn't true, because I have never done anything as rash as that and I have lived and played to regret it. Not that I didn't want to leave Blackburn Rovers. I did. My time there had run out. I simply chose the wrong time to put in my request, which attracted a lot of sensational publicity and I was accused of wallowing in it.

If I ask people who say they can remember my so-called rebellious days for examples of what they mean, this is the only instance they can remember, the only incident which stands out. It is still in my bones my one mistake, yet you only have to look at the state of that once great club, twenty years later. To repeat, my timing was out. But people tend to overlook that I was only twenty-one years of age, an age of indiscretion.

I like to think that over my years in the English League and the time before that in Northern Ireland, I have evolved as a footballer and as a person deeply and passionately involved in the game at other levels.

It is a game in which you are 'old' at twenty-eight, over the brink at thirty and almost a freak if you are still playing

16

at thirty-five, when the Grand Old Man order is bestowed by the sports writers.

I have always said that the most difficult years for any sportsman or sportswoman are between seventeen and twenty-five. This is when the prime is reached, when potential is fulfilled and when body and mind are the most active. It's also the period of troubled adolescence, when self doubt can undermine confidence and any display of self-determination can be taken as arrogance. It's a time of adjustment as well as exploration. If you can get through this period without too many traumas, the rest ought to be plain sailing.

I now look on myself as 'seasoned' and remarkably lucky that among the many injuries I received in my career none was severe enough to do more than put me out of action for a few months.

There are times when it's like going over the top, battling against obstacles and seeing others fall either side while you hope and pray that fortune or fate will be gracious and let you reach the final objectives. Scores of players are cut down in their prime or before, with broken legs, crushed bones, cartilage trouble, twisted knees, arthritis, . . . and rank bad management. It is the most insecure profession imaginable and to think that I survived in it for eighteen years makes me want to check the record books to see if I really did stay the course all that time. It seems like eighteen months. My memories of initial hesitant and apprehensive days at Fratton Park are just as vivid as immediate recollections which in this book I have tried to grasp and pull in; pulling together my experiences and analysing them.

What does it mean being a footballer in the second half of the twentieth century? I hope the following pages will go someway to answering the question. At least, it is my way, as a player who learned that there is a lot more to the game than kicking a ball about on Saturday afternoons, between 3 pm and 4.40 pm.

Two

The future, as the American humorist Mort Sahl used to say, lies ahead. It has been lying ahead ever since I came into the game. Everything they say will come out right in the end. The trouble with time is that it is a long time coming. If that sounds Irish, it is not so in my experience. We live in a slow-moving country, which explains why we have fallen behind other countries in the economic league table.

Slow and steady was once a national virtue, exemplified by Drake finishing his game of bowls before scattering the Spanish Armada (in fact, he had to wait for the tide to turn and was just filling in the time).

Today, life is quicker. The race is to the quick and the slow get left behind.

Football, as a profession, is too slow moving off the pitch. Our legislators seem unaware of the need to match their own thoughts and action with the game as it is played. They drift along, from one season to another, either unwilling or unable to introduce the sweeping changes needed to modernise the game's administration and make it more professional.

When I came into the game I quickly became aware of defects and deficiencies in the system. At the time I thought they were so glaringly obvious, they would soon be put right. Now that I have gone out of the game, as a league player, I find they remain almost the same.

There are three main issues in particular, that require urgent and immediate attention, three defects and deficiencies that drag down the game and prevent players and spectators from enjoying the fast moving spectacle that would bring back the crowds to those grounds where many attendances have slumped.

They are: the offside rule, the professional foul and the advantage rule.

Let me deal with them in order:

18

Offside: This rule is so obsolete it ought to have been abandoned long ago. It is negative, irritating and infuriating, to players and spectators. I used to argue for its restriction to the eighteen-yard area, but now I am totally convinced it should be swept away entirely. A side which resorts to the offside trap is confessing that it has run out of ideas and is too insecure to give the other side an opportunity to play open football. One example of how the offside trap can destroy the fluency and rhythm of a game is Liverpool *v* Spurs on 17 November 1979. Admittedly, any side going to Anfield feels apprehensive. The atmosphere is overwhelming, but a visiting side should respond to this as a challenge, not embark on defensive tactics designed to frustrate the home side. Spurs played the offside trap relentlessly and Liverpool fell into it thirty-one times! Not that it did Spurs any good in the end. They lost 2–1, I'm glad to say.

There are endless examples of the iniquity of this system. Another is the Leeds *v* Bayern Munich match in the 1974–5 European Cup Final, May 28 in Paris. Leeds scored a masterful goal, from a direct shot, which would have put them in a good position to win the match. But because Billy Bremner was technically offside, in no way interfering with play, a perfectly good goal by Peter Lorimer was disallowed. The Leeds supporters and players were enraged and rightly so.

Our legislators should have seen these incidents as a dramatic exposure of the fallacy of the offside rule. It might have had some value under old styles of play, but in these times of fast, open football it is an anachronism and a blight on the game, causing frustration and impeding strikers in full flight. Every time the offside flag goes up, thousands of spectators sigh and feel cheated. It is a shackle that should be cast out of the game.

The 'professional' foul: Of course, there is no such thing. There are only fouls. But we all know what the phrase means. It means a player nearing the penalty area, being brought down to prevent his scoring, in the belief that to give away a free kick is better than letting an opponent break through with a scoring chance.

Like the offside rule, the 'professional' foul just outside the area angers spectators and the side on the receiving end. The player who is brought down is twice penalised. Having been robbed of a scoring chance, he and the rest of his side now have the opposition lined up against them for the free kick. Having broken clear of the opposition, apart from the player or goalkeeper who has brought him down he now has to confront the entire opposition again.

What can and should be done about this? Some people say the referee should send off the player who has committed the foul. There is a more effective way of ending the 'professional' foul and that is to award a direct kick at goal from the spot where the offence is committed, with only the goalkeeper to defend the goal. In effect, this would be a penalty kick from outside the area. Players would be encouraged to sharpen their shooting and defenders would not be so willing to risk fouls a few yards or inches outside the eighteen-yard area. Another effect would be to eliminate at a stroke the aggrieved reaction of the players and the teams who have been unfairly penalised.

The advantage rule: Whatever happened to it? It's there, in the book, but how many referees apply it to keep games moving? Precious few. While the crowds shout for the advantage to be given, the referee blows his whistle, players are halted in their tracks and the ball has to be brought back for a free kick when it might have ended in the net. Usually, there is no advantage at all in awarding the free kick, which gives the opposition again time to close ranks.

Too many referees are whistle-happy and seem to think that any sort of foul demands the stopping of action for a free kick. If they are quick minded and intelligent enough, they should take in a situation at a glance and let play continue, if it is to the advantage of the player fouled.

All this strikes me as simple commonsense. Unfortunately, the game's legislators appear to regard certain rules as sacrosanct. They have not had the experience of playing the game at professional level. They don't know what it is like to be a player and I wonder if they really understand the feelings of spectators. If they did, they would not hesitate to abandon the offside rule, introduce direct kicks for 'professional' fouls and instruct referees and linesmen to make full and proper use of the advantage rule.

In my own time, changes have been minimal, though the

game has changed in formation. When I joined Portsmouth, in August 1957, the old orthodox line-up was still in operation – two full-backs, three half-backs and five forwards. Talking to young enthusiasts today about two-three-five and you might as well discuss warfare in terms of Great War trenches. He will ask: How did defences cope? What were the forwards doing when the ball was in midfield? Ah, but we didn't have midfields in those days. There was something called the centre of the pitch, but that was where the teams kicked-off – and there was a point midway between the centre circle and the goal where the incredible hulk, the centre-half, stood his ground, defying any attacking player to get past him. He was usually a hard nut to crack and the best way to beat him was to pass the ball out to a winger to make ground down the wing and then put over a centre.

Over the years I managed to adapt myself to the new systems without suffering any real loss of form. Changes are quickly absorbed, so the football authorities need not worry about altering the structure of the game if they make the radical amendments I have put forward.

That's how it was in those days. The trend over the last fifteen years has been to make players more fluent, doing away with the old fashioned winger and inside forwards. Players are now inter-changing and the game has become more like five-a-side football. In five-a-side the aim is to attack as a unit and defend as a unit. Hence, the phrase 'total' football has emerged; (if you want to give anyone credit for this word why not the Dutch International team? – they have perfected it better than anyone). Played at the right tempo it can be exhausting, and exhilarating. Today the jargon is that we are all players and numbers are irrelevant. Inevitably, the middle of the field becomes clustered with bodies.

Sentimentalists, and there are a lot especially in Fleet Street, recall the days when wingers could pause and rest on their wings. Centre forwards had time to stand around the centre like flagpoles. Full-backs stuck like glue to the rival wingers. Wing halves were the only players who took throw-ins. Like the stolid centre-half, they have all become obsolete. Why did all this disappear, to be replaced by the all-purpose formations we accept today?

21

A major contributing factor was the success of Alf Ramsey in England's 1966 World Cup win. He had no room for conventional wingers. If he had been England team manager ten years before and taken that view of wingers he would have had to rule out the likes of Stan Matthews and Tom Finney! This is one of those imponderables which makes the mind boggle. I'd leave it to the reader, young and old, to reach his or her own conclusion.

Alf Ramsey demonstrated his thinking on a world scale and he won a trophy to justify his decision. When a team is successful, nationally or internationally, its style is copied and its techniques enter the copybooks. Three clubs brought this new style to near perfection, Leeds for almost a decade, Arsenal for the best part of four years and Liverpool. Many clubs in the four divisions have tried, but they did not have the players to carry out the instructions. There is a moral here. Never go to war without the right weapons and the manpower to use them to full advantage, as the Israelites proved in 1967. It would be misleading to give Sir Alf all the credit. To be accurate, he was a precipitator through circumstance. Changes take place according to the law of evolution. Like changes, styles change, fashions change, so it is inevitable that the very game which reflects so many of the social aspects of society, should also change. In fact, changes often occur without many club managements being aware of them.

Take one example. At Leicester, a few years before I arrived there from Peterborough, Frank McLintock wore the no. 4 jersey. His style was similar to Billy Bremner's at Leeds. He was a busy player, all over the place, blessed with tireless energy and ability. In the same side was the up-and-coming Graham Cross, in the no. 10 shirt. He was a little ponderous and as play went on he would drop back into a defensive position. By wearing these numbers they confused the opposition. What they did wasn't planned. It just happened naturally. Liverpool later did much the same with Tommy Smith at no. 10 and Gordon Milne wearing the no. 4 jersey. Bill Shankly would probably tell you otherwise.

Unfortunately, there is a malaise rampant in football called copying. If one bright spark has latched on to something, others try to copy him. What begins as an innovation, or a piece of

22

original thinking, is soon used as a mould and facsimiles appear. Processing takes place and originality is lost.

Most football managers and coaches study their rivals. They do so to prepare their own sides, feeling they have an advantage if they know what to expect. But at the same time they are exposed to their rivals' patterns of play, which they can assimilate without being conscious of the fact. The seeds are planted, or rather they are scattered about and take root around the country. It is very probable that ideas drifted into Alf Ramsey's mind around this time as he watched teams in preparation for the World Cup competition. (Ironically, he did use two wingers at Ipswich during their successful period, Jimmy Leadbetter and Roy Stephenson. The problem with any sort of success is that it is followed by leaps on the bandwagon and in the process many managers and teams fall on their faces.)

I remember vividly Freddie Cox, when he was manager of Portsmouth, trying to do something different on the pitch. His idea was to bring Pompey's wingers back in deep-lying left- and right-half positions whenever the team lost possession of the ball and to revert to the normal wing positions when the ball was regained. It took the Portsmouth players some time to get the hang of it before the scheme was actually put into operation. For a while the opposition was confused, but we could not capitalise on it. In the end, the system fell down because of the inability of the players and the management's persistence with it even when the system was not working. Perhaps the management was too proud or obstinate to admit it was wrong.

Although I was not in Freddie Cox's good books, and our relationship was one of mutual antipathy, I have to admit it was a good plan. If he had had the right players to put it into effect, the results might have been striking and, of course, other teams would have copied it. Alf Ramsey had a plan when he managed Ipswich. Purists said he had such a collection of old players that there was no way he could win the league championship, but Ipswich were champions in 1962.

In my early, formative years, there were many players, myself included, it was said, who went through games without breaking sweat and coming off muddy grounds with shorts and jerseys clean. There is a romantic view of the past which insists that everything was better then, that players in the old days

23

knew more about the game than today's players. Some would find the modern pressure too great, with all the non-stop running and the exacting routines of training. I remember in one game how a defender marked his man, and after a goal was scored against his team, he would deny responsibility if the scorer was not the person he was marking. 'He's not my man!' he would say, in the days when no. 4 marked no. 10 and no. 5 stood in the way of no. 9.

Players today are fitter than those of the past. They have to be, to survive. Whether they are mentally atuned is another matter. It takes a lot of concentration and aptitude to adjust to new and increasing pressures. When I went with Wolves to America in May 1967 for ten weeks, I was glad to get home to a slower tempo. American life was twice as fast and hectic and I wondered how people there were able to relax. Two years later, on returning to the States, I found that there was not much difference in tempo. We were catching up and today, we are neck-and-neck. Pressure is on all the time. We are told that productivity must be increased, that our markets must expand, pay awards depend on productivity schemes, children in school have to learn more and learn faster, language laboratories attempt to teach in a few months what was spread over five or six years in previous generations.

We have no time to stand and stare ... get on with the job, hurry, jostle, get off the narrow road on to a motorway, the age of all systems go, why ground coffee when you can buy instant? Don't stroll, drive by car to the corner shop ...

Automatically, we adjust, but mental breakdowns are frequent. There are pills to put us to sleep and pills to keep us awake. Some people even take tranquillisers with their orange juice.

In the social atmosphere of the times, when so many strikes are really explosions of pent-up energy and an underlying resentment against the pressure of daily life, it is amazing that footballers are so well disciplined. Flare-ups on the pitch, no matter how much they are dramatised in the newspapers and on television, are rare. John Richards, whose sending off in the 1973–4 season I discuss later, is a good example. Football is not a world apart. It doesn't exist in a vacuum. It reflects the world around it, which is why the modern game has

24

changed in style and performance and why it arouses so much emotional involvement among so many people.

Just as more technical knowledge is required of people in a modern society, so more expertise and skill are demanded of footballers. Society is becoming increasingly bureaucratic and this trend is reflected in football becoming more methodical, with greater reliance on teamwork than on the individual player.

The danger is that too much method can inhibit creativity and an excessive stress on endurance and stamina can thwart individual flair. This has led to a lack of 'characters' in the game, players who combined individual skill with their own styles and eccentricities on the pitch. The sort of character I have in mind does not respond to conformity and stereotyped methods. He is best left to get on with the game in his own way; Peter Knowles before he became a Jehovah's Witness, springs to mind as a somewhat erratic but gifted individualist.

Too many managers are set in their ways and don't know how to let individual players express themselves. They impose on them their own ideas instead of stimulating their own particular talents, using players as ciphers.

Just before the 1974 World Cup final I asked a couple of managers if they were going to Germany for the event. I was startled by their reply. 'What for?' they said. 'We'd learn nothing there.' This attitude indicates what is wrong with the game. The same sort of managers can hardly wait for the next FA course, so they can go on what they call a 'refresher course'. Too many try to adapt players to their own styles and ways of thinking. This really stems from the profession's basic insecurity. Only a handful of clubs are financially solvent and most are worried about the next financial statement. When people are worried about insecurity, emotional and material, they are less inclined to experiment and be adventurous.

Throughout my career I have come across managers who haven't been able to accept the fact that players are capable of thinking for themselves and that they can have constructive thoughts. They have been so conditioned by the past, they have looked on players as hired hands whose job is to play the game and leave everything to those who are supposed to know best!

The attitude most of the time is: 'What's it got to do with you? You're only a player.'

But it is the players who make the game what it is. It is the players the crowds come to see. Point this out to some of the game's managers, legislators, and administrators and they will react as though you were an anarchist, trying to wreck the foundations of a game that in many ways has not changed for a hundred years. It does not follow that because the game itself has changed in style and techniques since 1966, its administration has changed accordingly, or correspondingly. It hasn't. It still clings to feudalism and Victorian paternalism.

There are some managers who believe that the ball itself is superfluous in training and bring it out only for practice games. If this attitude goes unchecked, the game could stultify, leaving the championship to be a contest between Stereotype United and Prototype Athletic.

I have an ingrained suspicion about coaching. It is not the be-all and end-all of the game. In the final analysis it is only for those who need it – and a natural player does not need much of it. I have never had a coaching lesson and I have known many players who, like me liken it to painting by numbers.

In my view, it is best to let young boys develop their game in their own way and to concentrate on the basic skills. It is no use trying to coach them into being 'a total footballer' if they cannot trap the ball, head it, make accurate passes or perform neat overhead flicks. I have said to coaches: 'But he can't head the ball or trap it,' only for them to reply: 'Oh, but you should see him run off the ball and find space for himself.'

It is bad enough to have this overdue concentration on football with a ball, let alone the jargon that goes with it!

I am often asked, because I have been associated with the game for so long, 'where is it all leading?' In other words, how is the game likely to develop over the next ten or twenty years? I'd like to make a definite prediction, but I can't; football is continually changing, just as a match itself changes and one can never predict the run of the ball. All one can expect is the unexpected. If it were otherwise, the game would be boring.

It is one of the least democratic (perhaps THE least democratic) profession in the country. It is still a profession which treats players like cattle, to be sold on the market, to be herded about and to be kept in place. Some of the 'beasts' are highly prized, of course. At an auction the best can command excessively high purchase prices. But a player with a £1,500,000 price tag around his neck – like Andy Gray – is no different, in spirit, to the player who does not rate in the transfer market. They are brothers under the skin and want the same out of the game – satisfaction. Transfer fees cannot buy satisfaction. Only the game itself can do that, for it's on the pitch that a player really lives, his skill, his stamina, his sense of purpose and his expectations, come together in an emotional crescendo. The game can take a lot out of a player and put a lot into him.

In my time I like to think I've put a great deal into it and now that I've finished playing I want to feel that I can still do so. One of the greatest tragedies of professional football is that the game lets go many of those whose experience could benefit it at all levels. It is absurd and unjust that a professional player while he is still playing cannot serve on the Football League Management Committee and FA Council. The FA represents his profession but he cannot represent his colleagues on that august body, though an amateur player in the same side could do so, simply because he is an amateur. It's the old gentleman-amateur and artisan-professional caste system still at work. Various reports on the game, most notably the 1968 Chester Report, and the CIR report of 1974, have commented on this state of affairs and made recommendations to change it, but all these farsighted, probing reports have been noted and pigeonholed, as if they were never meant to be more than sops to the conscience of the game's administrators.

But how would I like to see the game develop? That is another question. I would like to see managers and coaches encouraging players to develop their skills far more than they are able to do under the present system, which often restricts players to the wrong positions and can negate an individual's positive approach. I would like them to have more confidence in their players and encourage flair. There is too much fear of the unknown, too much timidity and playing safe when there should be more adventure and experiment. The game needs to be opened out and dragged from midfield stalemate back to the wings, where there is more space and man-for-man marking is impractical.

For a while, I would like managers and coaches to subordinate their own authority and back away to give players time and scope to develop new ideas and restore basic skills. While they (the managers and coaches) are breathing down their necks and yelling from the sidelines to keep to set patterns and stereotyped roles, there is no chance to try anything new and become more creative.

When players are given freedom, the results can be astonishing, as Brian Clough has proved at Nottingham Forest with his gifted winger, John Robertson, who has opened out defences and provided plenty of those 'killer crosses and runs' which thrill crowds. Nottingham Forest's success under Cloughie shows what can be done when individualism is combined with attacking teamwork.

It is easy to see what is wrong with the game and not so easy to put it right. Goodwill is not enough. There are too many vested interests and die-hard beliefs pulling in opposite directions. Much has changed for players in the postwar years, especially since the ending of the maximum wage in 1961 and the setting up by some clubs, such as Arsenal and Liverpool, of pension schemes for players when they reach the age of thirty-five, which helps to remove much of the uncertainty and insecurity that trouble players. I am convinced that a major factor in Liverpool's success is the club's welfare system and the security it offers to players who only leave in exceptional circumstances. Given this security, players are more at ease to concentrate on their game.

The biggest change is 'freedom of contract', or a qualified form of it in a package deal drawn up by the PFA and the Football League. Basically, all it does is give players some equal rights with their counterparts in other professions. Some managers and boards of directors have fought it, protesting that it can only damage the game, which is what they said about the ending of the maximum wage and say about any radical change that actually improves the working conditions of footballers, who are no longer content to be treated as hired hands.

If I had not been convinced that freedom of contract would

come, as a basic civil right, I would not have continued as chairman of the PFA to help see through delicate and protracted negotiations. It is the most important piece of legislation proposed by the PFA in its history and although it may not mean much to people outside the game, because they take such measures for granted in their own lives, it means everything to the 2500-odd members of the PFA.

If I had voiced some of my opinions and judgments expressed in this book, while I was still playing, I would probably have been accused of 'bringing the game into disrepute'. This is a stand-by phrase, a useful clause for those in authority over us to evoke when they want to protect their power and deny a player's right to speak for himself.

The game is sometimes 'brought into disrepute' not by maligned players, but by those whose decisions are taken without consultation with players and whose attitudes inhibit progress.

29

Three

To get to my vantage point, it's necessary to go back and trace my route. Life is a set of montages. That is how it seems, looking back. Memories crowd the mind, formative influences compete for predominance. Fortunately, I have never fallen prey to nostalgia, that sentimental turn of mind which softens and falsifies the past. I have been too busy living my life, concentrating on the ball at my feet or going to meet it in the air, to wallow in what has gone before. I prefer to help shape history than read about it. Having lived in England for twenty-two years – more than half my life so far – I have no claim to being a 'professional' Irishman, clinging to grass roots in Ulster, to justify myself. I became 'anglicised' long ago. But I have never lost contact with the side in Ulster which thrilled and elated me when I was a boy and which has been an inspiration to me over the years.

If I had not seen Glentoran play in the late forties and early fifties, when I was at an impressionable age, my sense of football, the equivalent of what the poet W. H. Auden called a 'sense of theatre', would not have developed. The two had much in common, because football is dramatic and has a relationship with theatre. I won't labour the connection. It's enough to say that the hours I spent watching Glentoran dramatised my feelings about the game to such an extent that I carry with me today a vivid impression of the players, especially the forwards. I have only to close my eyes, switch on a built-in mental projector and run my recording to my heart's content.

There is Sammy Lowry dribbling his way down the wing, cutting in, past one defender, then another. They can't impede him. He's too quick, too elusive. On you go Sammy. The ball is yours. He passes it inside to Tim Williamson. Now there's a scientist for you. That's right. A scientist with the ball. He experiments with it, makes it obey his theories. Whoever heard of a scientific footballer? I knew of one, this player, Tim Williamson. Now Dado Feeny has the ball. He's squaring up to a shooting position. Wham! The ball – where's the ball? Ah, there, in the back of the net. And the goalkeeper never saw it flash past. Now the game is in motion again and Sammy Ewing is bringing the ball down with his chest. The ball is magnetised. It floats to his chest. He lets it fall gracefully to his feet and it is his to command. A lob to Sammy Hughes, who meets it with his forehead. No juggler with plates could do more tricks than Sammy Hughes heading the ball. Here they are, five super-players, different and in complete harmony; diverse talents fusing with a striking force. Do I exaggerate? No. I am only putting into words now exactly what I felt then. And still do.

Almost thirty years later I relish my golden hours watching Glentoran. I don't remember them playing to any particular system. If they did, I was not aware of it. I was aware of their individual skill and the way they complemented one another. They had the right chemistry. Perhaps it was through sheer chance that they came together at the right time. Each was a player in his own right. None was a cog in a wheel. They had a blend which is rare, but when it occurs, guarantees success and excitement for spectators, like Real Madrid in the late fifties and early sixties, the Brazilians in 1970, the Dutch in 1974, and Argentina in 1978.

Managers and coaches strive, often in vain, to find this magical combination, this blend of skill that leads to fame and fortune in European competition, national, and international trophies.

My recollections of the Glentoran Five is that they played not primarily for the prizes, but because they enjoyed playing. Football was their life, their means of self-expression and yet they were part-timers. They had other jobs. Football was not the be-all and end-all of their lives, except when they were playing it. Many people who saw the recent BBC 2 programme 'Maestro', must have been surprised to learn that Tom Finney, now running a successful plumbing business, remained a part-timer, with Preston North End, throughout his career.

When Tottenham had Terry Medwin, Terry Dyson, Danny

Blanchflower, Bill Brown, Dave Mackay, John White, Bobby Smith, Jimmy Greaves, Les Allen and Cliff Jones in the squad, they had the kind of composition which could not have been bettered.

How could Manchester United fail when they had three world class players in the front line? Bobby Charlton, George Best and Denis Law. If only one of them 'turned it on' a match was virtually won.

Five or six players can form a nucleus of a successful side. Leeds, under Don Revie, had eleven – Norman Hunter, Paul Reaney, Terry Cooper, Paul Madeley, Billy Bremner, Johnny Giles, Mick Jones, Allan Clarke, Eddie Gray, Peter Lorimer, Jack Charlton. No wonder they dominated the first division for such a long period.

But it's not enough to have good players. Nor is it enough to have the right blend.

A manager has to create the environment for them to operate out of. All the streamlined coaching in the world won't make a scrap of difference if the players don't have what it takes. If they have it, a manager's job is to nurture and stimulate it. I simply say the right combination is 'players and workers' and if a manager and coach gets the players to work and the workers to play, you have it!

My search, from the beginning of my career, was to find a combination in which I could contribute to the chemistry. It was an odyssey which really began at Mersey Street School in a Protestant district of Belfast, where I was born.

I have often wondered if I would have developed my sense of football had I shone at classroom subjects. It could be that a deep involvement in the game at its 'lowest level', making do with rags tied in a bundle and kicked about waste ground, was a way of compensating for seemingly lagging behind in academic subjects – a deficiency I've tried to make good in later years through self-education.

Or was it my strong and abiding interest in football that swayed my mind away from other subjects?

Whatever the motivating factor, by the age of ten I was so deeply involved in the game it was already becoming a way of life.

Instead of reminding me to get on with my work and not

32

spend so much of my time out of school kicking a ball about, there was a teacher who went out of his way to encourage me. Mr Mawhinney must have seen something in my determination that convinced him I had the right kind of potential. If it had not been for him I might easily have developed a guilt complex about spending so much time practising football, when other lads were doing homework.

Few sports people who achieve anything claim to have done it all unaided. There is usually someone in the background, more often than not, a teacher, who has proved to be a lifetime's inspiration. I have heard British, World and Olympic champions say they were encouraged in their early days by teachers, fathers or other relatives; someone who saw in them particular talents that needed to be brought out, Mary Peters paid tribute to her coach, Buster McShane, who died prematurely; Sebastian Coe owed much to his father's influence and Steve Ovett was inspired by his parents and coach. If Borg's father had not won a tennis racquet in a raffle and given it to his ten-year-old son, would he have become a tennis champion?

The only place we could practice was in the streets. My own street, Avon Street, which sounds picturesque but was a typical back street of Victorian terraced villas, had a patch of waste ground at the bottom end; known sarcastically as The Meadow where I spent my Sundays, from early morning, six or eight hours. A few lads would start a game and as the day went on others would join in until there were fourteen or fifteen a side. It was rough stuff, a hurly burly, but I learned how to avoid crunching tackles and how to use my initiative. Sunday School was an interruption, rather like a long half-time break. I had to change into my Sunday suit, my only one, and best shoes to go to Bible class, then I would be back at the Meadow.

At the time, of course, I did not question the boundaries of this world in a poor district of Belfast. Nor did I realise how poor we were. I hadn't travelled and so I did not have a sense of comparison. What we had, which was little, was taken for granted. What we did not have, we did not think about. It's only when I look back, that it seems to have been a struggle. We just lived – and life was making do with the surroundings. I was, after all, a product of these surroundings and did not react against them until I had left them.

So it went on, until I left Mersey Street and attended the Belfast Technical High School. If I hadn't gone there I would have had to leave school at the end of the winter term in March and so would have been disqualified from playing for the Northern Irish Schools International team. It's strange irony that to continue playing football I had to take a course in woodwork, science and French, along with the other normal subjects.

In my year at the technical school I played against Wales in Cardiff, against England at York and Scotland in Belfast, this extending my horizons and giving me an appreciation of soccer 'across the water'.

By this time I had decided on making a career in football. It did not happen straight away. From the high school I got a job in a toy factory but it went bust later on. I then followed my father into the Harland and Wolff shipyard as an apprentice electrician.

In East Belfast there is a tradition similar to sons following fathers down the mines in the Rhondda. The shipyard looms large, but though I went in as an apprentice electrician my heart was not in the shipyard. My only reason for going was to please my mother. She thought I would be 'safe and secure' there learning a skilled trade. My grandfather and uncles had worked there and it was taken for granted in the family that I should do the same.

I had no more idea of how to be an electrician than playing rugger. I went through the motions but my mind was on soccer.

There was no sports centre in the district at that time but there was a good boys' club which encouraged football. This was Cregagh Boys' Club, which listed George Best among its members, though I was some years ahead of him. Boys' club football was taken seriously in Belfast and I took advantage of it as a route to Distillery which I joined at the age of fourteen. The year before I had signed for Linfield but they did not take much interest in me so I left.

I shall never forget my sixteenth birthday, playing my first game for Distillery against Glenavon in the Irish Cup. I had had a number of third team and second team games at centre forward or inside left. In the first team I was at centre forward, I didn't like playing in this position, but when you make your debut you are happy to play anywhere in the side. My favourite

34

position was centre-half or left-half. To this day, I still regard myself as a makeshift centre forward!

In that year my mother died, of cancer. This severed much of my kinship with Belfast. She had been the centre of my life there and now she was gone I felt no pull from the grass roots. I wanted to get away. My occasional visits to England, for trials with Preston North End and Bury, had convinced me of the need to play football full-time and make my living from the game. At that time part-time professionals earned £6 a week from the Irish League.

Eighteen years later, when I went back to Belfast to inaugurate the Northern Ireland Professional Footballers' Association in May of 1975 the maximum wage was still only £6 a week. Not much had changed in Irish football. Even if there had been full-time professional football in the province in my youth I would have wanted to leave. I left as if the city were closing in on me. I was restless, anxious to extend myself and welcomed the opportunity to join Portsmouth after a number of other clubs, such as Wolves, Blackpool, Leeds, and Glasgow Celtic, had shown an interest in me through their scouts.

Eddie Lever, the Portsmouth manager, must have been impressed when he saw me in a midweek game against Bangor, though I didn't play at all well in the 1–1 draw. The following Saturday I was at inside left against Newtownards and I had a fair game. We beat Newtownards (Ards) 3–0. I managed to hit one from over twenty yards (from time to time I did) that went flying into the net. I wondered how H. P. Davies (Old International) at the *Guardian* would have described that shot. Anyway my game evidently convinced Eddie Lever I was good enough for the English League, first division.

Such is the exuberance and callowness of youth that when I boarded a ship for Heysham, on the first stage of my journey to Portsmouth, I was in a Walter Mitty state of mind. I had visions of immediate fame and fortune, my talent setting the English League afire. I was going to have a startling impact and everyone would soon be talking about 'this bright new player from Northern Ireland'!

At the same time I was apprehensive about what to expect at Fratton Park. I was not going straight into the first team. My

35

place was in the reserves and it was only through an injury to Ray Crawford that I got my chance at centre forward, making my first-team debut against Manchester United at Old Trafford in October 1957. I had detested the position in the Irish League and had no desire to make it my permanent position. I have always thought of myself as a defender, but fate was deciding otherwise. Not that I was an automatic choice for Ray Crawford's position. They tried all other likely contenders until the final choice was between me and the groundsman!

It was then that I first realised the terrible insecurity of professional football. Ray Crawford's broken ankle caused him to lose his position, to me, later they got rid of him to Ipswich, for a pittance.

In my first season I was included in the Irish World Cup party and I made my full international debut, in Sweden, against Czechoslovakia, at the age of nineteen.

Life was not so rewarding though at club level. Results fluctuated and we just struggled to avoid relegation. Eddie Lever, a considerate manager, was replaced by Freddie Cox. It soon became apparent that I had nothing in common with him. All at once I felt insecure.

During Eddie Lever's management I had been very happy. Supporters responded good-humouredly to some of my more extravagant antics on the pitch. One or two ponderous sports writers accused me of trying to make a showbiz personality of myself, but this was never my intention. I simply thought the game could benefit occasionally for a little light relief. Under Freddie Cox the atmosphere changed.

Even a well-established player can get a shock when a new manager arrives and makes it plain that his face no longer fits. Talent is not always the issue. Clubs are not run by talent alone. Personality plays a decisive part in team selections. Some managers, like some teachers, have their pets, their blue-eyed boys who can 'do no wrong', even when they are doing everything wrong on the pitch. This points to a basic insecurity in managers themselves. They need a player, some chosen favourite, to boost their self-esteem. It is not usually the individualistic player they choose, but an ordinary, mediocre one, who is anxious to please 'the boss'.

If a player's face does not fit there is nothing he can do about it. He can 'suck up' but it won't make any difference. All he can do is go, uprooting himself and his family. Ten or more years' service with a club will not weigh at all when the new manager works out his own balancing act.

Sometimes the face might fit but not the style. A new manager has his own ideas and if a player's style of play is not what is expected from now on, the result is the same. Stay and linger in the reserves or leave.

There was no possible way I could get on with Freddie Cox. We were worlds apart and as long as I stayed there was bound to be a collision. Eddie Lever had respected my views and judgments. He gave me faith in myself as a player. All he lacked as a manager was a hard-driving instinct and some luck, which is essential in a competitive game.

Under the Freddie Cox regime, small matters became crises, niggling worries were magnified and I thought there was no longer a sense of proportion at the club. I was on edge and tended to over-react, which probably convinced the manager that I had to be kept in check. One day I received a letter from the club asking why I had changed 'digs' which had been arranged for me. Freddie Cox called me to his office and demanded an explanation. As I saw it, there was nothing to stop my changing accommodation if I felt I would be happier at another place.

He took the view that I had to live where the club directed. I told him that if the club were willing to pay for my accommodation all well and good. If I was paying the bill, which I was, then it was for me to decide where I lodged. I could see that he had made up his mind I was a rebel. I was challenging a system the club had operated without question for a great number of years. He just could not understand why, unless I was determined to be difficult, I should want to defy the system. It was useless my trying to explain that away from the club my life was my own and I could look after my own accommodation arrangements. I was not going to tolerate being treated like someone being sent to an approved school. After all, I was not an apprentice. I was a fully-fledged international player, Norman Uprichard and I were the only current internationals in the side. But in my experience at English League clubs, selection for England is all that counts. Some English managers

37

do not attach much importance to players chosen for Ireland, Wales or Scotland. For many of them, it is like playing for a pub team or a works outfit and they tend not to regard the selection of players for the also-ran home countries as adding much, or anything, to their clubs' prestige. Regretfully, some of the English pressmen share the same attitude.

It is very important for a young player to have good 'digs' where he feels reasonably at home. In my novel, *The Footballer*, I described a house where apprentices were looked after by a landlady approved by their club, running the home like an institution, with all manner of rules and regulations and few real homely comforts. This typifies some of the 'digs' I have known and heard about, where landladies are in effect 'spies' for the clubs and report to the managers whatever apprentices do.

Clubs have a responsibility to the parents of young players in 'digs' and need to assure them that all is well. But there is a difference between attentive landladies and surrogate matrons, who look on the youngsters in their charge as juvenile delinquents. At Portsmouth I was old enough and responsible enough to find my own lodgings and I resented the club's interference with my liberty. Eventually, I did find very good digs.

Nothing seemed to go right at Portsmouth. Old supporters there are probably still chuckling today over the Freddie Cox master-plan. At a time when the orthodox formation of two full-backs, three half-backs and five forwards was still in vogue, he came up with a revolutionary system of three front runners. The new system was rehearsed in pre-season training and six weeks were devoted to it, before he decided we were ready to unleash his 'secret weapon'. News of it got into the Press and supporters were curious to see how it would work out in practice.

Three days before the match in which our three front runners would pulverise the opposition, the new system was dropped. The order came to revert to the usual system and forget what we had rehearsed. It seemed there was a failure of nerve and Freddie Cox had decided to play safe. The result was a 2–1 home defeat, by newly-promoted West Ham, in August of 1958. But the system we had practised was resurrected later in the season.

38

Away from the pitch, most of the players were irritated by petty restrictions, such as being forbidden to drive to the ground and told to walk for the exercise. I used to drive and park my car in a nearby side street. On Friday evenings one of the assistant trainers was instructed to call at the players' digs to make sure they were tucked in and not out enjoying themselves in the town.

Far too much control was being exerted over us and it had nothing to do with discipline. This was disciplinarianism. Players need to discipline themselves and if they can't, then their clubs should disown them. It is futile for clubs to draw up rules which govern them when they are away from their clubs.

It is like being allowed away from a ground on parole.

At Portsmouth I could not stand this personal interference with the implied suggestion that we were not capable of behaving ourselves without supervision. My arguments with the management gave me the reputation of a trouble-maker.

On match days I forgot my grievances. The Fratton Park crowd appeared to enjoy my style of play and my occasional idiosyncracies. Not so a local sports-writer who took me to task in an open letter and went on to tell me what was good for my game. He judged me as a clown and failed to see that my antics were 'extras' and that I was still taking myself seriously as a player.

I indulged in carefree antics only when we were winning and in a good position. When we were losing I felt I could not afford to relax sufficiently to make the antics pleasurable. He that plays the fool must first prove he can play the king.

Life was not so amusing off the pitch at Portsmouth FC. There were times when only the high spirits of Norman Uprichard, the Irish International goalkeeper, kept up our morale. I have never known a player with such an incorrigible sense of humour. He was one of J. B. Priestley's 'gentle anarchists', a man whose special delight was deflating the pompous and never seemed to be upset or demoralised when things were going against him. Just the kind, in fact, to be at your side in times of adversity or in a crisis. He was a familiar character all over town. Norman must have had a happy childhood because nothing could shake his high spirits, not even being told to report under the club's disciplinary procedure (when he got on

39

the wrong side of Freddie Cox) for special training by himself in the afternoons.

Life at Portsmouth for me had its ups and downs. A high point came in February when my broken ankle had mended and I was fit enough for the first team. I was taking out a girl who worked for one of the directors and she got much of the news about the club first-hand. I had been playing a few games in the reserves to get fit when she told me that I would be in the first team against Blackburn on the Saturday. The customary ritual was for the players to look in the local paper on Thursday evening to see if they were in the team as the teamsheet in those days did not go up until Friday morning, Freddie Cox would have been furious if he had known I'd been given the team two days beforehand – looking back I wish I had informed him, if only to see his reaction.

The club tried to live by the rule book and players were kept in line. What applied for one player applied for all. By the sound of it this was egalitarian, but in training it had ridiculous consequences. For instance, it was absurd to put me on weight training, this benefited some players but it only had a weakening effect on me. My physique was not meant for weight lifting, but because of the system at Portsmouth I was obliged to do it. I had no desire to be another Charles Atlas. Weight lifting was not in my line. All I wanted to do was to concentrate on sprinting and practice with the ball in training.

To substantiate this point, when Glenn Hoddle burst on to the international scene for England against Bulgaria on 22 November 1979, at Wembley, he scored in a dream debut. In the next forty-eight hours the pundits wanted to know how it all came about, considering the traumas he had endured at Spurs the previous couple of seasons when he was in and out of the team. At one time, he could have been on his way to another club. Glenn explained to his astonished admirers that he was criticised by the management at Spurs because he drifted in and out of games and was not consistent enough. So he had done something about it. He had added one and a half stone to his fragile frame in one year and now had the stamina he needed.

In his own words he now 'felt as strong in the last ten minutes as he did in the first ten minutes'.

The only difference between him and I, is that it took

me twenty years to go from eleven stone to twelve and a half stone.

It may sound arrogant, but I have always known best, what was good and what was bad for my game, or my training. If other players on the books had similar notions they kept them to themselves. There was a great deal of dressing-room bickering, no one had the courage or the audacity to take complaints where they belonged, to the manager's office. I first noticed this reluctance to 'speak up' not long after arriving at the club and being involved in a dressing-room inquest on a defeat. The chairman wanted to know what was happening and no one dared to speak up. There was a player who had won nearly fifty international caps and he was looking at the ground. I don't now remember what I said, but I spoke up and the looks of astonishment from the other players made me feel I had spoken out of turn. Expressions revealed what some of them were thinking: 'Who does this Irish upstart think he is?' Some of the lads at any club say a lot after a defeat, among themselves, but when it comes to the inquest not a word is spoken.

Dissatisfaction with the club could have led to my asking for a transfer. As it turned out I didn't have to bother. I got a message at my digs asking me to go to the ground. Mr Cox was unusually affable. 'Blackburn Rovers want to sign you,' he said. I was overjoyed. It did not matter to me that Blackburn was way up north. I knew little or nothing about Lancashire, which was represented to me by George Formby films I had seen at Saturday matinees in Belfast. I'd have gone anywhere to get away from Freddie Cox. It was not that I disliked the town. Portsmouth was a pleasant, healthy place in which to live, but the manager could not satisfy my ambitions and I didn't think I'd ever be able to express myself there, even if I'd stayed for ten years. Normally, the only way a player could get away was to ask for a transfer. I just had to get away. It never crossed my mind that I could be jumping out of the frying pan into a Lancashire hot pot.

Looking back, Portsmouth evidently did not recognise goal-scorers when they had them! Freddie Cox, the manager, let Ray Crawford go before me. Between us, at different clubs, over the years we went on to score more than 500 goals, mostly in

41

the first division but I doubt if we would have notched that figure if we had stayed with Pompey.

There was some poetic justice in my move to Blackburn, which followed a goal I scored against them at Ewood Park. It was my first goal after my broken ankle had healed. I wonder if there is any connection between players moving to clubs against which they have turned in goalscoring performances. Another instance which comes to mind is Frank Munro becoming a Wolves player shortly after scoring a hat-trick against us in the final of an American tournament in Los Angeles on Friday, 14 July 1967.

My two seasons with Blackburn Rovers were marked by a number of goals, but my career there has been reduced to one isolated incident – my request for a transfer on the eve of Blackburn's FA Cup final against Wolves. More than any other event in my career, this confirmed me as a rebel and set off a chain reaction that made it hard for me to convince clubs and managers that I was not a rebellious trouble-maker. It was futile for me to point out that the Cup Final was not the occasion for my request, but coincidental and that at the time I simply wanted to get away, regardless of the final at Wembley. After a year at Ewood Park I had asked for a transfer because I was not settling down in the north and had been told by Dally Duncan not to be silly and realise I was with a good club. I had to agree that the club had a tremendous forward line in Bryan Douglas, Peter Dobing, Roy Vernon and Ally Macleod, but the conditions at Blackburn were no better than those at Portsmouth and when my written transfer request went in, just before the Cup Final, I was unfairly castigated as a publicity-seeker.

I realise now, with hindsight, that my timing was unfortunate and my request, in the circumstances, was an insult to a club on its way to Wembley. If I live to be a hundred, I shall always regret my action, but any young man in whatever walk of life, needs the right environment to inspire him and I did not have this at Blackburn. Neither Blackburn Rovers nor Portsmouth were run as well as Distillery and training – if you could call it that – was a bad joke.

With hindsight, I must admit that I did a double disservice to Blackburn by posting the transfer request on the morning of

42

the Cup Final and playing in the Cup Final when I was not fit enough, due to a pulled leg muscle at Birmingham City's ground the week before.

Vanity was at the heart of my pretence that I was fully fit. Come what may, I did not want to miss the Cup Final. I wanted it to be my moment of glory. I visualised myself scoring the winning goal. In the event, we went down 3–0 to Wolves, and we could not even claim a moral victory. If I hadn't played and a fitter player had taken my position – well, who knows? It might have been different, and then again perhaps not.

In the summer after the Cup Final, Dally Duncan's management ended. In my opinion he possibly had a raw deal. His departure meant my staying, because without a manager there was no one to ask if another club was interested in me.

The chairman asked about my grievances and I told him I was not happy at Blackburn. I also told him that it would be in the club's interest to let me go. There was no virtue in having an unhappy player on the books. He did not see it that way and insisted on my staying. So I decided to give it another try and in the first match of the new season I scored a hat-trick against Manchester United at Old Trafford. I continued to score goals and was happy playing without a manager. In my renewed mood of confidence, I was happy to 'give it another go'. Then along came a new manager, Jolly Jack Marshall, whose arrival coincided with my decision to withdraw my transfer request.

He was a funny sort of bloke – and I do mean funny. We called him Jolly Jack because he was always joking. You would go to his office with some niggle or problem and before you knew what was happening he'd be telling you the latest joke and you'd forget what it was you had gone to talk to him about. But life was not altogether amusing. I didn't see the funny side when I was fined £2 for an 'act of disobedience'. The money was refunded when I protested, saying he was not allowed to touch my wages, but I was suspended for a day which meant that I would be £3 worse off than if I had accepted the fine. The suspension was fixed for a Wednesday, the day we had the morning off or played golf. I had a better idea. 'If I'm going to be suspended,' I said, to Jolly Jack, 'let's make it a Saturday.' He didn't call my bluff.

43

There were plenty of other disagreeable incidents, some of them trifling, but all of them discordant and underlying my conviction that Blackburn Rovers was not the club for me. I quite liked the friendly nature of the people in the district. They accepted me and I had a few friends, who compensated for the drab surroundings. But I had a nagging belief that the club was trying to humiliate me and most of the players. At the end of the 1960–1 season the PFA under the guidance of Cliff Lloyd and George Davies, had been successful in negotiations with the Football League to get the maximum wage abolished. To my indignation the club offered me terms less than those of some of the reserve players. This was the last straw – and I reckoned I'd have to be as docile as a zombie to accept them.

The letter offering me what I took to be unrealistic terms infuriated me so much I tore it to pieces and threw it on the floor of the secretary's office. My gesture was followed a few days later by the offer of better ones, but it was too late. Life could never be sweet for me at Blackburn. I was on my way to Birmingham. Gerry Hitchins, idol of the fans at Villa Park, had been sold to Milan. Aston Villa needed a replacement. They came for me, paying £15,000. They had got £100,000 from Milan for Gerry Hitchins. A few cynics said that Villa were buying £15,000 worth of trouble, but Joe Mercer, one of the most amenable managers in the game, was willing to take a chance.

Time and again I have been asked why I moved from one club to another with such regularity, in two-year periods until I reached Molineux. At the time I put it down to restlessness, but what caused that restlessness? It was not a simple desire for change, a fickle attitude to club and environment. It was, as I see it now, with hindsight, a deep-seated craving to find freedom of expression. Football is an expressive game, drawing on a player's personality. What supporters call 'style' is the player's self-expression. You can tell at a distance, from the back row of the stands and terraces, what a player is expressing, though you cannot see his face. There is something in the way he moves, the way he kicks the ball, the way he moves in and out of positions, that identifies him and distinguishes him from other players.

At Portsmouth and Blackburn I felt stifled. In a short time

I knew I had gone as far as I could go and if I stayed, I would deteriorate – I was just turned twenty-two but a player knows his time is always running out in football. I did not know then how long I had to go in the game. All I knew was that you are an 'old man' in your late twenties. In two clubs in the English League I had not found what I was looking for and I was getting desperate.

Four

All the time, as I look back on my playing career, I try to assemble in my mind what I have learned. There is time now, time to reflect, time for considered judgments, time to think. Playing doesn't give you much time. Most afternoons are free for a player, but he doesn't really have time to sum up because he doesn't have time to unwind. The game is too fast. Its pace becomes the pace of his own life, off and on the pitch. When one game ends there is the next one taking shape in his mind, then the next. In the 1971–2 season I played more than seventy games, including testimonials and friendlies in front of paying customers. Some players, not many, classed as stars or superstars, learn to live with the pressures and order their lives to absorb them. Others find self-control difficult and the pressures too great. They don't like being singled out in crowds, nudged when walking through stores, besieged by autograph-hunters and garden fete organisers. It's one thing to get to the top, another to stay there and keep one's balance. What frustrates a player more than anything else, and what is most likely to upset the balance of his life, as well as his play, is belonging to the wrong club and not knowing what club would best serve his style and purpose. Worse is knowing intuitively which club is the ideal one for him and being unable to join it. This is the greatest problem in the game.

Clubs differ fundamentally. Just as no two persons are exactly alike, so clubs differ in temperament, outlook, atmosphere and features. A dud player at one club could be a star at another and vice-versa. There are probably scores of players with the wrong clubs, scarcely aware of their need to change and develop their talents elsewhere. Many are 'trapped' for private reasons, having family and business commitments in particular areas, and so play out their careers in relative obscurity. And they can also be trapped by the iniquitous transfer system which keeps them tied to their clubs.

46

There are also players who exhibit special talent with particular clubs and mistakenly convince themselves and other managements that they can take the same qualities with them wherever they go. They might be shining for lowly third or fourth division sides and then, pitched into higher division football, they fade and fail to make the grade.

It's of vital importance for a player who respects his talent and is aware of his capacities and limitations, to get with the right club. The club, that is, which matches his personality and style.

A player might have to ramble on until he finds his ideal stomping ground.

Clubs get their sense of direction and their styles from their managers or should do. Managers come and go. In my time I've played under twenty or so managers at club and international level. Only a few seemed to understand me and gave me the encouragement I needed. Not that I was exceptional in this respect. I have known managers who had their own notions of how the game should be played and expected all players on the books to conform, whether they had the capacity to do so or not. Individual talents were brushed aside in the interest of managerial dogma. It caused restlessness and frustration, disappointment and bitterness. Instead of understanding this the managers concerned behaved as if they, the managers, were being let down, as if they were being sold short and betrayed. I never ceased to be puzzled by managers. They have been players and in many cases they end up behaving like those very managers they despised in their playing days.

I'm the first to admit, especially over the last ten years, that managers are under continual pressure whether they are in the first division or fourth. They have to get results or be dragged to the chopping blocks. This means having to plan in a hurry to show what they can do in time for the next board meeting. Yet it takes time to build a successful side. It can take years of patient planning, searching for players, developing a confident style. I sensed potential at Blackburn and Leicester. The elements were there, but at managerial level, during my time with these two clubs, there was insufficient foresight. I don't want to do the managements an injustice. Perhaps they were nervous, just not good enough, or the job was too big for them.

47

In the end they were removed from office. I'd like to have been at boardroom meetings where these decisions were taken, and found out for myself how decisions were reached and whether directors really knew as much about their clubs as they liked to assert.

At Leicester I told Mr Len Shipman, that this was my ambition and I was not joking though he thought I was. (Eventually at Kettering I did attend boardroom meetings as a Pooh-Bah when I was chief executive.)

Blackburn had the nucleus of a very good team. In fact, the forward line was probably the finest I have experienced as a player. And yet the potential was not properly explored. It was allowed to deteriorate and since I left the side has toppled into the third division, making a spirited come-back to the second divison in the 1974-5 season; then slipping back again to the third.

Directors must accept the full responsibility of allowing a break-up of players at Blackburn and Leicester at times when the sides could have been powerful forces in the first division.

Football is a game of judgment which applies just as much off the pitch as on it. Without administrative judgment, players are left to flounder in limbo. Judgment is needed to assess a player, it is needed to appoint scouts who know what kind of young players to find ... It is needed by directors when they appoint a manager. All too often judgment becomes a hit-or-miss affair, determined by the mood of a moment, the look of a face or a whim. They are the ones who give managers long-term contracts one day and can fire them the next. Brian Clough arrived at Leeds on a publicity wave and the next thing we knew, he was 'washed up' at Elland Road, after forty-four days, but being made of sterner stuff than most managers he has bounced back at Nottingham Forest to silence all his detractors.

At Blackburn Rovers I had a marvellous first year and was made to feel at home in digs by an elderly woman, Mrs Crook, but I never had this sort of comfortable affiliation with the club. There was a gulf between players and directors. At times we were worlds apart. At my first two clubs I didn't know much about the directors, who remained aloof from the players. There is a tradition for this. It goes back to the last century

48

and the formation of the league. Directors are still seen as the patriarchs and players as the workers, belonging to different social groups. At some clubs players would no more think of 'trespassing' in the boardrooms than they would try to walk into the Stock Exchange. In return, they do not expect directors to enter their dressing room. It's an absurd, artificial division between parties, being broken down here and there, but generally operative throughout the league and resented by most players who have long since outgrown their serf status.

My early reputation as unreliable came through my refusal to be submerged by systems and pre-determined styles that would have stifled me. It was not bloody-mindedness that made me want to get away from Portsmouth and Blackburn; it was self respect. The least known tragedies in football involve talented players with the wrong clubs, too timid to get out and make a fresh start. They linger on, sink into self-pity and usually fade out of the game through deterioration in their play that would not have occurred if they had shaken the dust from their boots and found clubs suited to their style. Kevin Keegan is a good example of a player knowing not only when to move on, but where to go to further his career.

I learned in my youth to respect whatever talent I had and I had a raging desire to make the best use of it. This is the meaning of ambition. It can bring you into conflict with other players and managers, but if you allow them to beat you down to their level and their systems, you are lost. The moment a player knows for sure he and his club are operating on different levels, it is time to part company.

It's a pity more people, inside and outside the game, do not understand this fact of life. If they did, they would not be so ready to accuse players of disloyalty and fecklessness when they ask for transfers.

When I arrived at Aston Villa I lodged for a month at Joe Mercer's home before moving into 'digs' with Bobby Thomson in Wolverhampton. There was a kind of father–son relationship between us or so I thought at the time. At last, my career began to take shape, beginning with two goals for Villa against Wolves at Molineux. I woke each morning full of enthusiasm, eager to get to the ground. Early in the season Villa won the League Cup. Then came tragedy. A few hours after the League Cup

49

victory I was a passenger in a car with Bobby Thomson and a Wolverhampton *Express and Star* sports reporter, Malcolm Williams.

The incident, with its tragic consequences, led to rumours that we had been drinking and having a high time after the match. This would have been impossible. I did not play in the match, against Rotherham, because I was cup-tied. The match went into extra-time and did not finish until 9.45 pm and after the presentation on the pitch, it was after 10.30 pm before the players had come out of the showers and changed, which proved we could not have been drinking. Naturally, there was a lot of jubilation, which does not necessarily mean drinking, over being the first club to win the League Cup, which had just been inaugurated. We did not leave Villa Park until just after mid-night and then went to private premises for an hour. I had a couple of lagers there. Although it was getting late, Malcolm had to return to his office to write his report, so it would be ready for the early morning sub-editors and printers.

As we travelled through Willenhall, near Wolverhampton, the car in which I was a passenger, left the road, struck a tree and then hit a lamp standard. Malcolm, twenty-six, was killed. He had been sitting in the back and was thrown forward by the impact. He was dead before an ambulance could get him to hospital. It was a dreadful accident but had nothing to do with post-match celebrations. Malcolm had barely two pints of beer, as was later revealed at the autopsy.

For the next three months I was recovering from a broken arm and head injuries that needed over fifty stitches. Specialists advised me not to play again for six months. Joe Mercer argued against this advice, as he wanted me on the pitch – and he was right. I was back in action after three months.

I began playing again the second week of December 1961 and scored one of the goals in a 2–0 victory at Leicester. I was pleased by the way my game was progressing at Villa.

We finished the season in a respectable position. In the close season we went to Milan to play the Italian side, as part of the Gerry Hitchen transfer deal and beat them 4–1. I was among the scorers.

The following season began with three wins in a row and there were more tears of joy in Joe Mercer's eyes when we beat

50

Spurs at Villa Park, 2–1, and I scored both goals, in front of 65,000 people. Thousands were locked out. Our first four home matches of the new season attracted more than 200,000 spectators.

Confidence soared. We called for giants to fight, wanted mountains to scale and saw ourselves as football supremos, taking all before us. That was the prevailing mood at Villa Park. The adrenalin flowed. Everything I had imagined about Aston Villa was being confirmed. The greatness was not only there to behold, it was there to be experienced and enjoyed. No one had any doubt we had booked our position at the top of the first division. All we had to do was meet the payments, score the goals.

Then came the winter of our discontent 1963. I often wonder what would have happened had it been a mild winter. As it was, the weather was atrocious, snow and ice – I've never known a winter like it during my twenty-five-year playing career except for the winter of the 1978–9 season. A freeze-up suspended play for some ten weeks and this interrupted our continuity. It's an old trick, worked to perfection by some continental sides, to waste time by means of delayed goal kicks, feigned injuries and slow throw-ins, to upset the opposing side's rhythm. The weather played a similar trick. To make matters worse, I slipped on the ice in the street and twisted my knee, which prevented my playing and training and was to continue to plague me for the rest of my playing career. Even now, I have not recovered from it.

When I got back into the side after injury, I felt uneasy. The playing tactics had altered and I felt I did not fit in. I had become a stranger and as results went against us, it was clear the team needed a player to play up front with me, like Derek Kevan, of West Bromwich, who at the time could have been signed for £30,000. He was just the striker Villa needed particularly to form a partnership with me ... and I knew he wanted to leave The Hawthorns. Instead of signing him, Villa opted for West Ham's Phil Woosnam, a skilful and intelligent inside forward, but too cultured in his style when aggressiveness, as exemplified by Kevan was required.

I have always maintained that one player does not make a team but he can have a decisive influence and help to shape

51

a side. With the wisdom of hindsight, I can see where Villa went wrong in buying Woosnam instead of Kevan. The side had a cultured player in Ronnie Wylie, now assistant manager at Coventry, and needed an aggressive, physical player up front, to give me more support. With Woosnam the balance was wrong. I would not wish to detract from his talent. His particular skill was not what the side required at that particular time.

Bobby Thomson was a midfield dynamo and should have been played at left half, in the days before midfield play came into vogue.

He was wasted in a striking position, where he could not make the most effective use of his skill and in consequence, he had to take a 'lot of stick' from the crowd. They never realised he was being played out of his natural position.

Kevan and I would have made a formidable combination. If he had been put alongside me, I might have stayed at Villa for several years. The whole course of my career could have been altered – and I feel sure that Villa would not have plunged later into the third division.

This is why a manager needs vision and an ability to assess players not simply according to their own lights, but what they can do in a team. Too much 'culture' was the side's undoing.

Villa lost its rhythm and slumped to a long run of defeats.

We were knocked out of the FA Cup competition by Manchester United – I didn't play in any of these games – and beaten in the League Cup final by Birmingham, the cruellest cut of all!

Cardinal mistakes were made off the pitch, as well as on. The directors' decision later on to sell the club's idyllic training ground was a blunder. Financial considerations, selling the land for housing development, took precedence over common sense. I could have banged my head against the goalposts in anguish. Such folly only confirmed my view that boards of directors know too little about football and understand the requirements of players even less.

At Villa, I was on a see-saw – and I came down with a hard bump when I was made 'open to offers'. One sunny morning, during a training session, Joe Mercer took me to one side and said he had not meant to put me on the transfer list. 'Let's forget it,' he said. I could not forget it. My pride was hurt – and worse, I was losing faith in Villa, and Joe Mercer.

It seemed I was being blamed for the side's run of defeats. That was absurd. 'You know I was injured and didn't play in most of the games we lost,' I told Joe Mercer. I hadn't played in the FA Cup tie against Manchester United or in the League Cup final against Birmingham City. 'That's why I am blaming you,' said Joe, with twisted logic. 'Because you didn't play.' A left-handed compliment indeed! 'Contrariwise, said Tweedle-dee, if it was so, it might be; and if it were so, it would be; but as it isn't, it ain't.' That's logic!

I was stuck for words. My claret-and-blue blood began to boil. Was there, I wondered, more to all this than I was being told? There had been gossip about my social life, stories of night-club brawls, late-night hell-raising, girl chasing and general waywardness. Before Joe Mercer put me on the transfer list I decided to have it out with him and I went to see him at his home to ask him directly if he believed all those colourful and exaggerated stories and to sort out my position. 'No, of course not,' he said. 'I know they're not true.'

Looking back, I can clearly see I was utterly confused and did not know whether Villa wanted me or not. My confusion was increased when I was replaced on the team sheet for a match against Liverpool by George Graham, who was to make his debut. Why this sudden change of mind? A sports journalist, answered the question for me. He speculated on what the public reaction would have been if I, a player on the transfer list, played in the match and scored a hat-trick. What red faces there would have been at management level! What if I scored in other matches? Would they keep me on the transfer list or feel compelled to take me off it? The club told the press that I was unfit. To sort things out, I had two meetings with the club chairman, Chris Buckley, but he decided it would be wrong for him to interfere with the manager's decision.

It was obvious I had no future at Villa Park. It was sad. I liked Joe Mercer and still do. Perhaps I was too young and inexperienced at the time to understand him. I was only twenty-four. If I had been thirty things might have been different. I wish I had been a little older, mentally.

Supporters reacted angrily. There were hundreds of letters

53

of protest, some from season ticket holders threatening not to renew their tickets. At Portsmouth and Blackburn I desperately wanted to get away. At Aston Villa I wanted to stay, but they wanted me to go. My time was up. Three clubs in six years; three major set-backs. My buoyancy sagged. I was at a low ebb. If I could not make the grade with Aston Villa, then perhaps I was doomed. On the way out. Welcome to Skid Row Mr Dougan! I was ready to blame Joe Mercer, but it wasn't his fault. He was only reacting to circumstances and I had no divine right to remain a Villa player. Andy Gray found himself in a similar position before his move to Wolves much later.

Two events brought me back to reality. Living in the Midlands I had gained a reputation as a man-about-town. Many of the stories about my high living and sorties around the nightspots were exaggerated, but they had an element of truth. Not that there is anything unusual about someone in his early twenties kicking over the traces as money would allow. But the fact was that I was earning £40 a week before tax and paying for digs, there wasn't much left to indulge all the pleasures I was supposed to be enjoying, without running up a heap of debts, even if I had been able to live socially on credit. I used to borrow a couple of pounds from my landlady, Mrs Truman, in the middle of the week when I ran out of money.

I was dubbed a playboy, but that means a rich, pleasure-seeker. Well, I wasn't rich! Much of the gossip was exaggerated but some of it was true. After all, I was young enough to enjoy the company of pretty girls and I liked to frequent the popular hotels and night clubs.

I think public wish-fulfilment had a lot to do with my popular reputation at the time. On the pitch I allowed scope for a touch of showbusiness. The game, after all, is entertainment and a player is not an automaton. I have never understood players who pretend the crowds are not there and ignore them. Perhaps it's shyness. The Irish, by nature, are not shy and in the main they are more extroverted than the English. It was natural for me to play up a little to the terraces and stands, not an affectation. When the game loses its humour and there is no longer any room for what Wilfred Pickles called 'a spot of homely fun' then everyone might as well pack up and go home.

There was a popular story that when photographers were

taking action pictures of me in the goalmouth, the moment I heard a camera click or the purr of a television camera, I would hold the pose! My so-called antics on the field were enlarged in the public mind, off the field. Ah, well, the sports writers must have their day and dote on their chosen characters. Reputation is not what you are, but what others think you are.

There is a great deal of hero-worship in football and not only among young boys. Supporters of all ages have their fantasies, so when a player comes along and exhibits a playful personality either they identify themselves with him or fantasise his personality, making it more colourful and outrageous than it is. Sports reporters, on the look out for colour stories, seized on me as 'good copy' and people read between the lines what they want to read. Socially, my personality was inflated and I hardly recognised myself from the composite image that emerged. The likes of Brian Clough, Malcolm Allison, Bill Shankly, and Joe Mercer are good value for reporters who don't have to ferret too much. Some players too – George Best, Kevin Keegan, Stanley Bowles, Charlie George – are instantly newsworthy:

A bogus image could not sustain me when the walls came tumbling down at Villa Park. I felt hollow and in many ways an outcast. I remembered the thrill, tingling sensation, when Villa signed me from Blackburn. My move from the north to a nerve centre of English League football was more exciting than going to Buckingham Palace to receive a knighthood. Seventeen years later I still feel the same. Glory clings to Villa's claret-and-blue shirt tails. No matter how far the glory days recede into the past, eternal splendour gilds them yet at Villa Park. To be with such a club was an honour and then, within two seasons, to be rejected and told that only third division Peterborough wanted to sign me, was a crushing experience. My feelings were ambivalent. Part of me was full of despair, the other part full of determination to make an impact in the third division and prove to Joe Mercer and his aides that they were wrong to let me go.

My marriage, to a German girl, Jutta, gave me a new foundation on which to build my life at the very moment it seemed to be going downhill. The marriage had a decisive effect on my outlook.

Joe Mercer thought I was injury prone. I knew I wasn't. He

55

thought I was a luxury in a struggling side. I knew I wasn't. He thought there was substance in the rumours about me. I knew there wasn't. The misunderstandings made it impossible for me to stay at Villa. It was a shame because to me Villa was what the Old Vic is to an actor, Westminster to a politician and Mecca to a pilgrim.

The shock to my nervous system in going from the first division to the third was delayed. At first, I was simply glad to get away and anywhere would do. Peterborough was an unknown quantity but it wasn't the end of the world and I was something of a wandering minstrel anyway. Later after I had joined Peterborough, I discovered that a few other first division clubs wanted me. Most managers would rather a player go further down the league than 'promote' himself through his own efforts.

It was apparent to most of my critics and the sports writers that I was on the way out. Decline and fall in a couple of seasons. I am grateful to Peterborough and Gordon Clark. I knew before my first season began there that I had made a mistake in going to the third division when I was a first division player, and as I said, rather like an Old Vic actor joining a provincial Rep or a Westminster politician going into local politics. It was a jolt my senses needed. With the responsibility of marriage, I also realised the importance of getting back to where I belonged and not letting my career peter out in obscurity. It was no consolation to know I was the highest paid player in the third division. For me there was only one division, the first and I knew I could never be satisfied with less.

At least Peterborough toughened my sinews. The third division is mostly a physical division and any player who plays in it is sure to be strengthened. But if you have above average ability, there is only one division to play in – the first.

Peterborough was a sobering experience for me. I don't wish to underrate any of the players in the team. There were some talented and a few ambitious ones, as there are at any club, in any division. They deserved a higher brand of football and so did the town, which had expectations of promotion. The trouble with Peterborough United at that time was its hierarchy was 'non-league'. It had a non-league philosophy and was not geared, mentally and administratively, for higher

56

division football. In mitigation it has to be remembered that the club had been in the league only a couple of years when I joined them and the experience at the time was above most of their heads. There is a vast difference between the amateur and the professional, the full-timer and the part-timer, be it player, secretary or director.

In football you've got to think big before you become big. You've got to believe in yourself and then go out and prove you are right. But you can't always do it alone. In my time I have been indebted to various people, beginning with my teacher, Mr Mawhinney at Mersey Street School in Belfast. Maurice Tadman, Eddie Lever, Gordon Clark, John Ireland (the former chairman of Wolves), are among those who have encouraged, motivated and even bullied me. Players carry with them their experience, which is partly made up of what they have learned from others. It is a pity that more directors don't listen to players and gain from them the benefit of their experience. If the Peterborough directors had listened to some of their players they might have achieved what supporters expected the club to achieve.

Some players were keen to move forwards when the administration, in my view, were looking the other way, towards the fourth division. It was exasperating, especially when the incompetence was glaringly obvious and there was nothing anyone could do about it without starting a players' revolution. Small-minded restrictions and pettiness abounded. At no time did I get the feeling of a club on the move, streamlining itself for the great days to come. I wanted to play my heart out, as I had so much more to lose or gain and so did most of the players, but it was disheartening to remain a silent witness of unimaginative, stuck-in-a-rut boardroom thinking. It was a shame because the club had made its mark with giant-killing acts.

If Gordon Clark had not taken over as manager we all might have despaired. He renewed my sense of vocation, encouraged me when I was in low spirits and always reminded me that I was at heart a first division player. We were on the same wavelength, which answers those who say that I'm naturally antagonistic towards managers as a breed and want to do their jobs for them. Gordon Clark didn't try to turn out robots. He took a personal interest in his players as individuals and fashioned them into a team. With greater response from the boardroom he might have achieved more.

Football's greatest weakness is the reluctance or refusal of those who control it, to consult with those who play it. There's a deeply embedded prejudice going back to the last century, when 'gentlemen' organised the rules and footballers were the serfs or hired hands, the artisans whose duty was to impart their skill and keep their opinions, if any, to themselves. In the old days they doffed their cloth caps to the directors. These days, the class division has eased but there is still a gulf. In spite of articulate interviews on radio and television and sports columns in the press, players find it hard to persuade management, and directors, that they can think and talk constructively about the game and have ideas which, put into practice, could benefit the game at all levels.

One still hears the old cliché that footballers' brains are in their feet and they can hardly string two sentences together. The prejudice is exposed week after week, as players express themselves in the media, but it is deeply rooted and it will take another generation to overcome. It has been galling for me, as former chairman of the Professional Footballers' Association, which should be able to negotiate on equal footing with the game's other bodies, to find so many managers, many of them respected and successful, say that players ought to get on with what they know best – playing – and leave the rest to the administrators. As former players, managers ought to know better but at times they represent the biggest hurdle.

Five

When I have spoken up in the past, before I was elected chairman of the PFA, I've often been accused of trouble-making. The fact that as a young Irishman in the English League I might have views and opinions worth listening to, was unthinkable to those who had been schooled in the old days, like Matt Gillies when I was with Leicester, who said he did not want any 'dressing-room lawyers' when I told him I had been invited to serve on the PFA committee. It was easier for them to brand me as an upstart and an uncontrollable rebel than to pay attention to what I was saying and consider the justice of my pleas.

Even now, after chairmanship of the PFA gave me a reputation as a union negotiator, I have only to suggest players be given more participation in the running of their clubs and the cry goes up: 'Players' power!' I haven't advocated a players' take-over as a co-operative. All I have said and what I repeat here, is that if players and their association had been consulted in the past instead of being treated as inferiors by the other football bodies, the game's administration would not now be in such a pitiful state.

There are too many vested interests, clinging to the privileges accumulated in the past, still resisting the respect to which players are entitled. You can see this resistance at work in the managerial reaction to the PFA's freedom of contract policy, when it was announced mid-way through the 1974–5 season. One or two enlightened managers and directors took the view that it was inevitable, while others argued, without any evidence, that it would ruin the game, just as the abolition of the maximum wage was said at the time to be a threat.

Some improvements have occurred in the past twenty years or so, but 'players' shackles have only been loosened without being completely removed.

Players are trying to rectify mistakes made by our forefathers.

They have to overcome discrimination and the endemic attitude that footballers are lesser breeds without the law, subject to the will of their masters. The reaction 'What's it got to do with you?' when a player speaks up, has to be swept away.

If you see what is going wrong and have ideas of how to put it right and never say anything, then you become an accomplice in self-denial. I have seen players, anxious to speak up, cowered into submission because they know that whatever they said would be regarded as impertinent. I have seen players so much in awe of their managers that they've been afraid even to give a reporter a comment after scoring goals, like a Brighton player when he scored three goals but was forbidden by his manager (Brian Clough) to talk to the press. The player was approached after the match by reporters but he was shaking in his boots at the idea of being interviewed without his manager's permission. Even though his hat-trick was something to shout about, he dared not talk to the press for fear of Brian Clough, who does most of the talking for his players. He would not have gagged me! How could he adequately describe a player's own feeling after scoring three goals? That is something which must have escaped him – and the journalist.

The old system is still in force, not as obvious as it was in the past, but insidiously preventing players from enjoying what in other professions is accepted as fundamental rights. If I had taken to heart what I found various authorities inside the game thought about me, I would not have had the strength to go on. Fortunately, I was not encumbered by English reserve and I refused to be intimidated into accepting something I knew was wrong, to preserve my popularity with the Establishment.

Peterborough United was unlike any other club I had known. It had been made by the man-in-the-street who had chipped in to keep it going, when there was little enough money around in some areas for the basic necessities of life. I did not expect luxuries, but after the facilities of Villa Park I was unprepared for an almost entire lack of them.

The gymnasium was a small room under the stand and the training ground was a public park, with more dogs and dog-dirt on it than people. The ladies' tea-room pointed out to my wife with some pride on a conducted tour of the club, was reserved for the wives of directors, not the players' wives, who were expected to wait outside for their husbands after a match (later a storage room was turned into a small tea-room for them). Social conditions, which are important to players and their wives, improved when Gordon Clark took over as manager. Ground staff boys were brought in to look after our kit, card tables were installed in the coach taking us to away games and we soon began to sense that the new manager was 'thinking big'. But the more he did for the club, the less he seemed to be appreciated by the board. Within a year he had got rid of fourteen players and spent £30,000, a fortune then, signing new ones, including Vic Crowe, my former team-mate from Aston Villa. Ironically Gordon Clark had tried to sign me as a sixteen-year-old along with my great pal, Sammy Chapman, in 1955, when he was assistant manager at West Brom. Nine years later we were together.

What distinguished Gordon Clark for me then among other managers I had come across was his refusal to sign a contract. He said that in eighteen years he had not signed one. 'If they want to get rid of me they will and if I want to walk out I can,' he explained. He never kow-towed to directors and he put his heart into his job, with dignity and sincerity.

He deserved moments of glory and it came when we played Arsenal at home in the fourth round of the FA Cup. Arsenal had spent £250,000 on their side, managed by Billy Wright. They were held in awe and we had tried to model ourselves on them. They thought the match was a foregone conclusion and when eighteen-year-old John Radford put Arsenal ahead after forty-four minutes to lead 1–0 at the interval, they expected the second half to confirm their side's superiority. The Fen Tigers were in the bag! Seventeen minutes from time Arsenal supporters were singing 'When the Reds Go Marching In' – but their voices were silenced. Vic Crowe started a move down the line and Ron Barnes, the right winger, took the ball on. I dummied to go to the right of Ian Ure, dummied back again before taking a pass from Oliver Conmy to steer the ball past Tony Burns for the equaliser. Crowds surged over the pitch.

Four minutes from time Peter McNamee took a pass from Ron Barnes and tapped the ball into the net. It was the winner.

61

The roar from Peterborough's supporters must have echoed over the fens.

It is the usual practice for the home club doctor to visit the opposition's dressing room after a match to ask if there are any injuries. Our club doctor asked if any of the Arsenal players needed treatment for injuries. 'No,' someone said. 'Only eleven broken hearts.' Life in football is made up of these landmarks, the odd goal which proved decisive, the result which can influence a career ... I was sad to find later that this result was a nail in Billy Wright's managerial coffin at Arsenal.

Gordon Clark did not let the victory go to his head. A week later he told the press that it would take three or four years to get the club on a proper basis. Visions of reaching Wembley were dashed at Chelsea in the sixth round, we lost 5–1 and were cruelly brought back to earth. But for a while we had made the Posh a household name. The excitement of our cup run did not make me forget my determination to get back to first division football. When Leicester City came up with an offer which meant a salary cut of almost £1000 a year I had no hesitation in accepting it, simply for the opportunity to return to top level football and perhaps regain my place in the Northern Ireland side. Gordon Clark wished me well and urged me to take the opportunity. Although Leicester is only forty-three miles from Peterborough I did not watch a first division game in my two years at Peterborough. I just could not bear to watch a game in the division where I knew I belonged. I knew that at twenty-six I had to prove that I was not a has-been.

Leicester had a good, orthodox forward line and I welcomed having the likes of Sinclair, Goodfellow, Gibson and Stringfellow as my partners. I felt that after two years in the wilderness I was back home, among first division players. I don't wish to demean those third division players who made up the side at Peterborough, but frankly a player needs to be with colleagues of equal or greater skill to stimulate him if he is to achieve his best performances. It was not as if I had been a third division player making the grade in the first; I had slipped from the first division to the third, where I felt I did not belong although in my two years at Peterborough I found there were first division quality players playing in the third division – and when

I returned to the first division, at Leicester, I found 'third division' players playing in the first. It is up to a manager to sort them out but few managers have the ability to do so.

At first, I was grateful to Matt Gillies for rescuing me; then I realised that he was not totally responsible. It was my performances for Aston Villa against Leicester that had been remembered by Len Shipman who encouraged his manager to sign me. I had always done well against Leicester. At Easter, 1962, when at Villa we beat them 8–3, Gordon Banks, no less, was in goal. Bobby Thomson and I scored six between us.

If Matt Gillies had initiated the move to get me from Peterborough, his attitude towards me was curious indeed. He showed no sign that he welcomed me as a City player. Almost from the day I arrived there was an undercurrent which made me feel I was not welcome, as far as he was concerned. When I found out that the players were not being paid the same wages and that there appeared to be discrimination, favouring some and not others, I was very disappointed, but decided to stick it out for the sake of playing first division football again.

As I had taken a substantial cut in wages – nearly £1000 – to get back to the first division, it rankled to find out that I had been misinformed about all the players getting the same salary. They were not. But what can a new player do when he finds he has been deceived? Storm into the manager's office for an argy-bargy? I was glad to be back in the first division and not wanting to upset everything from the start, I let it go. So much for the theory that players are only in it for the money.

As I have already stated, I realised that Matt Gillies and I were on different plains. I found him remote and uncommunicative, while he in turn found me wayward and too self-determined. My impression was that he thought I had too much to say for myself and this made him suspect me of being potentially troublesome. It was clear that he had no idea how to handle me, because I did not react to him in the way most other players did. There was a small incident when we were going to Maine Road to play Manchester City, in an FA Cup-tie, which illustrates the antagonism between us. The club chairman's bag was waiting to be put on the coach and Matt Gillies told me to carry it. I asked him if the chairman was ill or something and could not carry it for himself. He repeated the instruction, which I refused to carry out. One of my team mates was then told to carry it and he complied. This must have confirmed for Matt Gillies that I was a threat to him. He didn't take too kindly to this. There was another incident on the train from Manchester after a cup-tie at Maine Road, when we were ordered to move to another carriage, so the directors could have our seats. We refused to move. He always seemed to me to be anxious to please his directors.

If I had gone to him and asked: 'Do you regard me as a threat?' he would probably have gone through his pork-pie hat in astonishment and asked me what on earth I meant. But there it was, in his attitude towards me, impersonal and suspicious.

Not long after I had joined Leicester City, the biggest compliment of my career was paid to me. Cliff Lloyd, secretary of the Professional Footballers' Association, invited me to join the PFA Committee.

Immediately, I went to Matt Gillies to tell him of the invitation and let him know I was keen to accept. Out of respect I didn't want him to read about it in the press. His reaction amazed me. 'I don't want any dressing room lawyers here,' he muttered. And this from a manager who had been a PFA delegate in his playing days at Bolton!

'What do you mean?' I asked, incredulously.

'I don't want any trouble in the dressing room!' What did he think I was, a Trotskyite or Marxist, plotting to establish a subversive cell among players?

I had always been a conscientious PFA member, never behind with my dues. It was an honour to be asked to join the committee. I thought any manager would regard the invitation as an honour for the club. Not so Matt Gillies. Or was his terse, uncongratulatory reaction due to *my* involvement? Would he have taken this attitude if another player had been invited?

If I had been a Scot, I have no doubt I would have been accepted by him. Leicester at this time had a reputation for being more Scottish than English. Perhaps he did not appreciate my Irish temperament. We had a lot of Scotsmen on the books. Five in the first team were Scots. It was a tradition going back to the forties, when I discovered that the club's signature tune was Johnnie Scobie.

64

Having been out of Northern Ireland's consideration while playing in the third division, I was now back, as a first division player, in the international side. Returning to Belfast, to play for my country against Scotland in October of 1965, I was full of apprehension playing at Windsor Park. I had yet to establish myself convincingly as an international player there and a great deal depended on the kind of performance I gave in my comeback. It could be make or break. It was a crucial match in my international career. My guardian angel did not desert me. We beat the Scots 3–2 and I scored a goal, with my right foot, the ball flashing into the net just under the crossbar. It still ranks in my memory as one of my most satisfying goals because of the circumstances and timing, and because I scored with my right foot.

As I have said, there were a lot of Scots at Filbert Street, and it was not surprising as Matt Gillies was Scottish. When I returned to the ground on the Monday, I expected to be kidded by them during training, which I was. Matt Gillies could not find it in his heart to congratulate me. He made some banal remark, which left me with the feeling that in being associated with Northern Ireland's victory over Scotland I had let him down. I felt then that my days at Leicester were numbered – though I was to remain another eighteen months – and that in the meantime only virtuoso performances by me would keep me in the first team. In spite of the distance between us, he never omitted me from the side. It was a side which, with proper guidance and encouragement, could have reaped glory. Instead, a process of decline and fall was allowed to accelerate. It makes me sad now to see what has happened to Leicester City. I wonder now if Matt Gillies and the directors feel the same.

Leicester had exciting prospects. There were only a couple of positions which needed strengthening, like the Blackburn side I had played in. One player who could and should have been brought to Filbert Street was Terry Cooper, who had not yet established himself in Don Revie's side at Leeds and was just the type of player to help pull the team together where it needed tightening.

When we played at Elland Road, Davy Gibson and I asked him if he fancied coming to Leicester. He said he would be more than interested. We spoke to Matt Gillies about him, but Gillies did not show any enthusiasm, although he could have signed him for around £25,000.

Strengthened by Terry Cooper, Leicester could have had a side to challenge for the championship, but as at Blackburn, the administration were apparently unaware of what could be achieved, given a little more effort, and as it turned out, Leicester settled for mediocrity while Terry Cooper displaced Willie Bell in the Leeds side – and it was Bell who went to Leicester, for a reputed fee of £45,000, a couple of years later. I have always said that one man doesn't make a team, but he can make a hell of a difference.

It is my opinion that Matt Gillies never appreciated his team and his judgment was questionable, as was proved when he transferred me and later transferred Gordon Banks to Stoke. The side disintegrated, without achieving anything and was eventually relegated.

Leicester City had become used to being an ordinary side. It was just not in the 'thinking' of the directors to be among the Arsenals, Liverpools, Manchester Uniteds and Leeds of the football world. There were ambitious players on the books who were keen to compete for the championship, but they did not get the backing they deserved and their efforts were unacknowledged. Talent was allowed to go to waste.

I knew that nothing was going to change and that as long as I stayed I would be stuck in a rut, just as I had been at Blackburn. It was said by Leicester that they had the best two years out of my career and that I was finished when I left, but I went on for more than another eight years and scored more than 120 goals in the first division for 'The Wolves'.

Six

Only the most starry-eyed, naive young player cannot be aware of these facts of professional life in the league. If he has confidence in his ability he accepts the odds and battles against them.

But there are other pressures, inconspicuous from the outside, and they can test a player's staying power just as determinedly as those he experiences on the pitch.

In the account that follows of my playing career with Wolverhampton Wanderers I have concentrated on the background pressures to show what can, and often does, happen if a player comes up against a manager with whom he fails to enjoy a mutual understanding.

A football manager is all things to all men, women, boys and girls who are associated with a club or support it on the stands and terraces. He personifies a club far more than the chairman or any of the directors, because he is the figurehead. He is the man on whom the club relies for success. Brian Clough proves my claim.

Managers do not come from a mould. They are not trained for the job and how they get where they are is usually a mystery, even to the 2500-odd professional players in this country. Much of the time, particularly since the war, they seem to be involved in their own game of managerial musical chairs, swopping one hot seat for another.

The constant changes can have unsettling effects on players who find themselves 'stranded' when the manager who has signed them departs and his successor does not favour them.

They may have found the club of their choice, only to find, overnight, that they are not the new manager's choice.

Frankly, there are not many managers in the game who by strength of personality, tactical skill and practical psychology command the respect and devotion of their squads. Many are

67

'led' by their own players and take the credit themselves for success and inevitably, pay the penalty of failure. But when this happens 'compensation' in the form of financial settlements can be enormous. Brian Clough's reign at Leeds was short, but he took away with him a fortune in severance pay.

More is written and said about football than any other sport in the world, perhaps more than is written and said about politics. And yet little is known about the game as it affects the daily lives of those who play it for a living. No one outside a club knows what goes on inside. Most professional clubs are inner sanctums, self-protected from outside scrutiny. Some may hold 'open days' for the fans who are ushered along the corridors, shown the dressing rooms, the physiotherapist's department, the trophy cabinet, locker room, gym and so on, then ushered out with a few autographs.

Sports reporters may call or phone for a statement about a player who wants a transfer or for an assessment of the next match. It's routine. Players train in the mornings, may play golf some afternoons, go on close season or pre-season tours, a mid-season break by the coast, take the wife out shopping.

If that were all, a footballer's life would be simplicity itself. Football is pressure – pressure to compete, to win, to get to the top, to stay there, to survive. Not all the pressure is confined to the pitch. It exists in the background, at some clubs all the time, and for some players it can become unbearable. Oddly enough, the big pressures are the easiest to deal with, because they are the professional demands which a player expects. They are part of the game, a game which thousands of youngsters want to play for a living and which has room for only a few.

The fall-out rate between the ages of sixteen and twenty-two is enormous and between twenty-two and twenty-eight it is also quite heavy. The average playing span of a player fortunate enough to graduate from schoolboy and apprentice to reserve and then first team, is only eight years. Having made the grade, there is no guarantee of keeping a fixed position, because there is always someone else nudging for it.

Players are under the constant commands of their managers. Some managers smile for the cameras and crack jokes for sports reporters, putting out a public face of charm and affability, then turn aside to treat their players like morons, without humour or sympathy. There are also indecisive managers and tyrants, nervous ones and bullies, easy going fellows and harsh disciplinarians. I have met all sorts in my time, co-operated with some, argued with others and found only two or three who appreciated what we, the players, were trying to do.

There can be no greater managerial contrast than Ronnie Allen, who signed me for Wolves from Leicester, and Bill McGarry, who succeeded him.

This is how it was at Molineux:

In 1969 I ended my first autobiography, *Attack!*, which took me up to 1967, with these wishful words: 'Some people say that Wolves' best days are gone. I prefer to think that the best are yet to come.'

A new manager, Bill McGarry, had not long arrived at Molineux from Ipswich, with a reputation as a hard-driving disciplinarian, who knew how to be tough and severe when he thought it necessary to get a team into shape.

The next seven years, under his reign, were the most traumatic of my career. They were years of torment, frustration and at times I came close to walking out of Molineux in a rage. What kept me there was the club itself, John Ireland the chairman and the aura that had lingered over it from the illustrious fifties, when Wolves took on the mightiest European sides and beat them. The glory had departed, but the footballing world had visions of it returning, if only Wolves could find the right style, the right pace, the right blend of attack and defence. We needed a new fighting spirit, a sense of adventure and an over-riding belief in ourselves.

It never happened, not as I hoped. The 'best days' I anticipated have not yet come. They would, if the right decisions had been made, the right players sought and bought ... but football is full of stories of what-might-have-been and never was. Chance plays a part, but more often success depends on shrewd judgment and flair, which in my opinion were not conspicuous managerial qualities in the McGarry years at Molineux.

Everything might have gone Wolves' way if Ronnie Allen had been given more time and not been so brusquely dismissed when he was beginning to form the nucleus of a powerful side. He knew how to buy and sell players, manipulating the transfer market to his side's advantage. Not that I have ever agreed with the transfer system, which in my view reeks of the cattle market and has brought many clubs to the verge of bankruptcy. I despise it, and as a former chairman of the Professional Footballers' Association, I have campaigned against it, in favour of freedom of contract for players.

If Ronnie Allen hadn't come along with £50,000 to complete my transfer, I might have stagnated and could easily have dropped out of the game before I had turned thirty.

When Matt Gillies called me to his office and told me that Wolves wanted to buy me, he gave me ten minutes to make up my mind. Later I asked Ronnie Allen why there had been so much rush, the course of my career having to be decided in ten minutes, which hardly gave me time to phone my wife to ask what she felt about another move. During negotiations it was revealed that Wolves had been trying for six weeks to get me. Subsequently I found that Jim Marshall, the late father of the present chairman, and John Ireland had as much to do with my coming to Wolves as anyone.

Poor Ronnie (though not so poor, while he was in charge of the Saudi Arabia national team). He was never given his due at Wolves and I have often wondered if this was because the partisans at Molineux secretly resented a former West Bromwich rival in charge. The 'feeling' between West Bromwich and Wolves is like that between Birmingham City and Aston Villa, or between Liverpool and Everton. It is not easy to cross over. It probably did not occur to Ronnie that he had to prove he was a Wolves man, which meant forgetting that he had ever played for West Bromwich.

At the time his dismissal was greatly unfair, most people thought it was due to the thrashing Wolves were given by Liverpool. Being hit for six, on home ground, was made more humiliating by two of the goals being scored by Alun Evans, whom Wolves had sold to Liverpool for £100,000. The score might have turned out differently if Wolves had taken advantage of an early chance to score. A high ball was pumped into the air and a Liverpool defender was about to jump for it just inside their half when I called, in a mock Scouse accent, 'Hey, leave it!' He checked himself and left it. The ball ran free and I latched onto it, haring down the right wing before cutting in

70

and squaring a pass over the goalmouth. Mike Kenning, running in, had an easy opportunity to score, but shot over the bar. Tommy Smith in the Liverpool defence was fuming and gave me a mouthful. 'That bloody Dougan, ref,' he moaned. 'He's always doing that.' He was right. It was gamesmanship. I did it mostly for fun and in our encounters with Liverpool I never failed to rile him, with this tactic.

Was the Wolves' board secretly pleased about that defeat? It gave them the excuse they needed to get rid of Ron. His card had already been marked and it made no difference when the following week we restored our pride by collecting two points at Coventry, where I scored the only goal. For five months the directors had been trying to lure Bill McGarry from Ipswich. This was not known at the time and was only revealed, years later, when McGarry was contemplating a move from Newcastle to Stoke.

Liverpool made everything that much easier, providing the six bullets that despatched him from Molineux. The defeat was a pretext, or an occasion, for getting rid of him; not the specific reason.

To some extent, I must concede, he brought on himself a little of his trouble. First and foremost he was a coach, a superb one. When he became a manager he needed a firm, right-hand man; someone to relieve him of the backstage grind he accepted as part-and-parcel of the job. He thought he had to be 'head cook and bottle washer'. If he had concentrated more on the essentials of management and a little less on coaching, he would have made his position more secure. A tough aide-de-camp might have given him the strength he needed to secure his position at Molineux.

I got on extremely well with him, not only because he had signed me, but because there was an easy rapport. He was a warm, articulate man, always friendly and approachable. We didn't always see eye-to-eye, but when we disagreed there was no resentment or any kind of rancour. For instance, I did my best to persuade him to buy Gordon Banks from Leicester. A successful side needs a top-class goalkeeper and I knew that Gordon was ready to leave Leicester.

There was no disrespect towards Phil Parkes, a teenager at the time and, like Peter Shilton, would have benefited

71

alongside 'a master'. He would have agreed that Gordon Banks was world-class. When I suggested an approach, Ronnie frowned and said: 'He's getting on a bit.' I said 'He's not yet thirty, only a year older than me.' 'Ah, yes, but you're different,' he said ... Years later when Wolves were playing at Tranmere on the 31st October 1973 in the League Cup competition, Ronnie came to see his son, Russell, who was playing for Tranmere. During a chat over old times I said to him: 'Your mistake was not buying Gordon Banks.' He paused, and said, 'Do you know, you were right.'

The chance was lost and shortly afterwards Gordon went to Stoke. He would be playing in the first division still but for that terrible car crash a few years ago.

On another occasion I was more successful in giving advice. During a tour of the United States, we played against Aberdeen, who had a formidable player in Frank Munro. There was some aggro between Frank and David Burnside when the two teams met in Washington. It began when Dave took a throw-in and the ball hit big Frank on the side of the head. He thought that the ball had been aimed at him on purpose, which it was, and he retaliated with a few well-aimed punches. Our pipe-smoking chairman, John Ireland, was sitting on the touch-line and in the interests of Anglo-Scottish friendship, not to say public relations in front of an American tournament crowd, he stepped in with his pipe of peace and tried to separate them, catching a few of the blows himself.

In the tournament final, in Los Angeles, Frank scored a hat-trick. So did Dave. The outcome, decided by a sudden-death goal, was a 6–5 victory for Wolves. Frank had done enough to impress Ronnie that he would make a valuable asset for Wolves when we returned home. But could he approach a player who had come to blows with one of his own players and drawn the club chairman into the bust-up? He was worried about what to do and in his office he asked me what I thought of this strapping six foot Scots lad. I had no hesitation in saying that he was a player of immense talent and he would do well to get him. I am not sure whether he counselled anyone else.

He backed my judgment and his own and went ahead with the signing. He had the satisfaction, in his long service for Wolves, of knowing that the club chairman never held the

Washington incident against him. For a reputed fee of £45,000, it was one of the best investments Wolves could have made.

Another player he talked to me about was Barry Powell, on the books as a fourteen-year-old schoolboy. Ronnie could not make up his mind about him, obviously because he bore little resemblance to what most people imagine a footballer should be, big and strong or sturdy. Here was a sprat and at a glance he didn't look much of a footballer. But in a five-a-side game at our Castlecroft training ground on the edge of Wolverhampton I did more than glance at him in action. I admired his control, his stamina and his subtlety for a kid. There was no doubt in my judgment that he was an embryonic Johnny Giles or Billy Bremner, one of those 'shorties' with towering talent ready to burst out, when given the scope. In all my years in English football I could not think of a young player who had impressed me more at fourteen years of age. 'Potential' was written all over him and I told Ronnie this. I don't know to this day if he discussed the signing of players or transfers with other players.

It gratifies me, having seen what Barry Powell has done for Wolves, Coventry City, and Derby County, that I had an eye for talent. To illustrate his stamina, a few years ago when Wolves were on a pre-season tour of Sweden, I set my mind on leading the field in a cross-country training run to prove I could still outrun them all. I was much older than the other players and prided myself on being able to keep ahead of most of them in training. To 'rub it in' I held back at the start to give myself a handicap of 100 yards and then one by one, I overtook them, until I came up to a bend and passed Steve Kindon (later acclaimed as the fastest footballer in the league). Another player called to me: 'Little Barry's in front.' I thought he was joking, as I could see no other player ahead. But when I turned a bend just ahead there was Barry at the finish, 100 yards in front of me!

I still believe Wolves should have clung on to him. He was still developing his full potential when they sold him to Coventry.

I say 'they' when I mean Bill McGarry, whose excursions into the transfer market fell far short of Ronnie Allen's and can only be described on the whole, during his period at Molineux,

73

as not too successful. Time and again he bought players who did not make the grade and had to be sold at a fraction of what he had paid for them, while others who might have been developed, with proper encouragement and insight, never fulfilled themselves in the side.

The arrival of Bill McGarry at Molineux on 25 November 1968 had a touch of farce, with an opening scene Brian Rix would have appreciated. All the players were assembled in the dressing room when suddenly the door burst open and in sauntered a small man wearing a tight-fitting, light-blue track-suit. In those days tracksuits were rare and the style did not leave much room for leg movement, so when he tried to raise a leg to put his foot on the seating which ran around the room, he missed and stumbled. Not to be deterred, he assumed a listen-to-me posture and declared: 'I'm the manager. I don't give two ... (expletive deleted, but commonplace on the terraces at most football grounds, except Nottingham Forest) if you don't like me. I don't want you to like me!' (Seven years later I was still taking him at his word.) He went on to say, in growling tones, what we were going to do. Some of the young players were impressed, even overawed.

It may seem blasé, but I had heard it all before, from other managers, especially at Portsmouth under Freddie Cox. They like to create an impression of vaulting ambition and they give themselves airs. The best just get on with the job. My first impression was that Bill McGarry was going to brow-beat us into success and did not mind being seen as a hard taskmaster. I thought of Bette Davis in 'All About Eve', saying 'Fasten your seat-belts, it's going to be a bumpy ride!'

If I had known how bumpy it was going to be I might have sought to get away. I had learnt you can get out without asking for a transfer. The contrast between Ronnie Allen and his successor was startling, which didn't augur well for continuity – on or off the pitch. But I did not try to sum him up on the strength of his introductory pep-talk, with his sergeant-major overtones. Events would take their course and everyone would have to adapt themselves to the new regime. As it happened, only one player made the transition with ease, the team skipper Mike Bailey, who from my early days at Molineux had kept his distance from me and was never noticeably friendly to me.

Bill McGarry's loyalty towards him may have been commendable, from a personal point of view, but there came a time when it interfered with the structure of the team and had a disastrous effect on a particular player, professionally.

I saw no reason after the managerial changeover to depart from my custom of offering advice if ever asked on how to strengthen the side by trying to get certain players I knew were available. Ronnie Allen had welcomed a number of my suggestions. Some managers and directors make a point of asking experienced players at their clubs for advice on players they are thinking of buying – and why not? Bill McGarry was less responsive and I had the impression that he regarded me as an Irish upstart, whose eventual aim was to run the club. Managers who are basically insecure are usually suspicious of players who take a close interest in their clubs.

They cannot understand that a player has only the success of his club at heart and is not trying to undermine his manager's job or trying to lay the foundations of player-power. Constructive suggestions can be, and are, interpreted as stepping out of line and life can be made awkward for a player as a result.

Professional football in this country has a long history of servility, with players treated as hired hands who are not expected to open their mouths off the pitch – except to say 'Yes boss.' Some managers and boards of directors are finding it hard to accept the fact that footballers today are more articulate and more professional than their forerunners of the cloth-cap era, when players were kept down and told what to do, with no decision being questioned or challenged. We are living in an age of self-expression in all spheres, except football.

I would not have presumed to make any kind of suggestion if I had made no particular contribution myself. As it was, I had managed to score nine goals in eleven games which enabled Wolves to clinch promotion back to the first division, with a hat-trick on my home debut against Hull, and I was enjoying a friendly relationship with supporters. I felt 'at home' with Wolves and was satisfied that at long last, after various moves – Distillery to Portsmouth, on to Blackburn, then Aston Villa to Peterborough and Leicester – I had reached journey's end.

Because of my history in moving from club to club the chairman, John Ireland, asked me after a few weeks how long I expected to play for Wolves. 'Mr Chairman,' I said. 'I'll give you ten years.'

There was speculation in the press when I signed, that I would soon be off again, after a couple of seasons, which had been the pattern of my career until then. In the event I fell short of the decade by just under two years, only because of a recurrent back injury and disaffection between Bill McGarry and myself. Later, I had to undergo major surgery on my back. If I had had the operation years ago, my playing career would have been extended. I now know I could have gone on playing until I was forty in the first division.

Wolves were striving to consolidate themselves in the first division after two seasons in the second. The first season after promotion is nearly always the hardest. Teams often rise and fall in successive seasons – Northampton, Huddersfield, Carlisle, Hereford, Southampton, Burnley, Sheffield United . . .

To gain promotion to the first division and before long win the championship, like Nottingham Forest, is exceptional. When a side wins promotion it is usually happy to consolidate, around the middle of the table. A side newly promoted has to be strengthened with new players, which is the secret (though it's not really a secret) of Nottingham Forest's success under Brian Clough.

Even when reliable players are needed to consolidate a side, it is tempting to let one or two regulars go if they can command high transfer fees and the club needs the money. I don't know whether Wolves needed the money they got from Everton for Ernie Hunt, but it was a good price – £80,000. His departure, however, left me feeling lonely in the attack and the situation was not helped by the rivalry, whipped up by supporters, between Peter Knowles and David Burnside. At home matches a section of the North Bank crowd would tease Burnside by chanting 'Peter Knowles!' and a rival section would raise the cry, 'Burnside!'

It must have got on David's nerves, because before a match against West Ham he made it known that he did not want to play. Ronnie Allen asked me what I thought and I said that in my view, if he didn't want to play, then he should be left out of the team. Alun Evans was brought in for his debut and played alongside me after I had told Ronnie I would look after

76

him. We won 2–1 and I scored both goals, the first made for me by Alun.

David Burnside was one of the finest ball-jugglers the game had known, but he seemed unable to reconcile his 'mental attitude' with his artistry. It was a great pity, because he had much to offer Wolves and the game at that time.

One of the most significant changes that occurred was in training. Under Ronnie Allen a lot of time was devoted to ball skills and five-a-side football. Under McGarry the emphasis was on the physical side. At least McGarry made Wolves the fittest side in the league, if not the most talented. Like the Scottish contingent at Leicester, Wolves players never spared themselves in training. There was a competitive spirit in training sessions, one player trying to out-do another and all vying for leadership. Bill McGarry not only demanded a fit squad, he always led the way himself, and was extremely fit for his age.

But the side needed strengthening if it was to repeat the glories of the fifties. People in and around Wolverhampton still spoke of the Championship and Cup Winning years as standards that had to be followed in the immediate future. Their folk-heroes were still Johnny Hancocks, Jimmy Mullen, Billy Wright, Peter Broadbent, Roy Swinbourne and my favourite – Eddie Clamp. In their collective memories they replayed the goals against Honved, Moscow Dynamo, Spartak and Real Madrid. (Just as I reminisced about my heroes at Glentoran.) They talked of the famous long balls, the devastating assaults down the wings and they were desperate for new glories to match the old.

I wondered if Bill McGarry ever sought inspiration from the trophies neatly stacked in showcases in the entrance hall. Or were they to him mere baubles of the past?

Before he had been long installed, a less convivial atmosphere began to emerge at Molineux. The general office was made out-of-bounds for all the players, though I noticed Mike Bailey went inside without being challenged. When Mr McGarry told me I could not use the general office, I asked if he meant me alone. 'Yeah, you and the rest of the players,' he said. Again, no reason was given. It was simply another instruction which no player dared query. There had been no trouble or inconvenience and as far as I knew none of the general office staff had complained about our calling in occasionally to collect mail or any messages, or to buy tickets for the game. It was an irksome restriction, one of many imposed during his reign.

One morning, as chairman of the PFA, I needed to speak urgently to the association's secretary, Cliff Lloyd. I knew he had to travel some distance from his home in Cheshire to his office in Manchester and that he did not arrive until 9.45 am. This was the time I had to be at the ground to be ready for training at 10 am. Anyone late for training was fined £5 to £10, then double that if they were late again. I needed to speak to Cliff Lloyd but I knew if I stayed at home to make the call I would be late for training. At 9.30 am I rang Bill McGarry at the ground and explained to him that I needed to speak to Cliff Lloyd on an urgent matter which could not wait until after training. He told me: 'You know the consequences if you are not in on time.' I put the phone down, muttered some unrepeatable remarks to my wife and hurried in my car to the ground. Instead of being able to make the call from the general office I had to change into my training gear and run to the social club, adjacent to the ground, and make the call from a public phone box there. If this was a way of demonstrating his authority all it did was make me more resentful and question his approach to management. It was no consolation that he did the same to other players. I considered this a mean way to treat someone with responsibilities towards a highly professional body which, over the years, had confirmed its status. There was no explanation for refusing my request to be a few minutes late for training and I could only assume that rank was being pulled.

Minor irritations can be unsettling when there is more serious business to attend to – and what preoccupied the players was the hard work needed to restore the pride and success of a great club which had fallen on hard times, having twice been relegated since the golden era, which ran from the 1953–4 season to 1960. The club had to re-appraise itself, to take stock in all departments, from the boardroom to the groundstaff. It needed to promote itself better and win back the crowds. There was still a hard core of supporters, who would always be there, no matter how high or low the club's position in the league.

78

Their loyalty had to be rewarded and there was no better way than to challenge for promotion or to win a major trophy; preferably both.

I did not see how this could be done without new players. We had the nucleus of a fine side, laid down by Ronnie Allen. He inherited Knowles, Munro, Holsgrove, Parkin, Parkes, Bailey, Powell, Taylor, Wagstaffe, Hibbitt and me without doubt, the nucleus of a good side. It was Bill McGarry's job to build on it. One player who might have had a strong bearing on the side, if he had been properly used, was Danny Hegan, who had played in McGarry's side at Ipswich and was bought in the close season of 1970 from West Bromwich. He was a little fellow with exceptional talent, one of those players for whom there had never really been any other job in life. He was meant to play football. He had a football brain and he knew how to transmit his brainwaves to his feet. He was not among the quickest of players and was better suited at going forward from a deep position.

When Mike Bailey was injured in January 1972 Danny took his place for the next five months at no. 4, his natural position. He figured prominently in the British home championships in the Northern Ireland side at the end of that season and was acclaimed the outstanding player of the series. This was Danny Hegan's heyday. He should have been kept in that position, which allowed him to control the pace of the game and set up attacks. But as soon as Mike Bailey was fit, Danny was given the no. 7 shirt again and no matter how hard he tried, he could not adjust to it.

Bill McGarry liked to play someone wide on the right and I believe this came about through Alf Ramsey's use of Alan Ball as a wide no. 7 in the 1966 World Cup Finals. At various times he tried Jim McCalliog, Alan Sunderland, Mike O'Grady and Kenny Hibbitt in this role. And he made the mistake of instructing Danny Hegan to play wide, when all his footballing intuition and ability demanded a more central midfield position where he could use his vision. He could see things, before they happened, far quicker than Mike Bailey, who, as he got older, was often caught in possession.

Supporters still talk about Danny's remarkable sixty-yard chip shot when Spurs' goalkeeper, Pat Jennings, was caught

79

out of position in the May 1972 UEFA Cup final. It ranked with Pele's chip in the 1970 World Cup final. I can give no higher acclaim than to say if it had been in a World Cup competition it would have been shown repeatedly on television.

When Danny himself was forced out of position he brooded. Wearing the no. 7 shirt and playing wide on the right side was a phobia for him and he felt he could not make an adequate contribution to the side. Although any impartial selector would have given Danny Hegan preference over Mike Bailey, there was no question of the skipper being dislodged. Loyalty is commendable when it is given to all players on merit and not confused with favouritism.

Unrest builds up under the surface when a manager favours one player at the expense of another. Ability alone should have been the criterion.

Personal problems were blamed when Danny went missing. There was gossip in the town about his being unreliable and indifferent towards his own career. The truth is that he knew he had done enough to justify himself at no. 4 but was being kept out by favouritism. When he turned up after one of his benders, before a midweek match, I made it clear to Bill McGarry that if he didn't play him he could ruin him. I am glad to say that he put him in the side, but the best of Danny Hegan was not brought out. It was allowed to stagnate and when he reacted by failing to turn up for training and being seen out drinking at different places in the early hours, he was on the downhill road leading to the point of no return.

His 'comeback' was an article in a Sunday newspaper, giving his name to sensational allegations about players' drinking habits. The last I heard he was a football coach at Butlins holiday camp. I hate to see talent fall away before reaching its fulfilment. Danny Hegan came into this sad category. Bill McGarry lost patience with the player's unreliable habits, but did not seem to realise that these were caused by his unwillingness to give him the role for which he was so admirably equipped. It was as if Tommy Lawton had been put on the wing and Stanley Matthews given the no. 9 shirt. What would that have done for both of them? Danny Hegan's promising career at Wolves was cut short by forces beyond his control.

A different kind of force, a religious one, cut short the career of another talented Wolves player – Peter Knowles. Even without a lot of talent he would have still been an idol of the girls and young boys who supported Wolves. Tall, fresh complexioned and unpredictable, he carried with him an air of jauntiness and impetuosity that girls usually find attractive in a young man.

He had great talent and was admired by those who look more critically at a footballer in action. Although he could be erratic and inclined to let a sudden flare-up of temper on the pitch upset his judgment, I am quite sure he would have matured sufficiently to have played himself into the England side. I visualised him as a future England regular but when he was converted by a Jehovah's Witness on the doorstep of his home, he was unable to reconcile what he took to be a religious calling, with his chosen profession.

It was a sad day for Wolves and for English football when he decided to quit and devote himself to his new faith. At the time he explained that he was turning from the game because he feared he might do an opponent serious injury in a game he claimed was being ruined by foul tactics and clogging. It was impossible to plead with him that he was over-stating his case, or that it was quite easy to remain a Jehovah's Witness and play professional football. He was adamant that the two, for him, were irreconcilable and some power on high was leading him by the hand away from Molineux to the promised land he was convinced would follow the ending of the world a few years later.

The world didn't end as he predicted, but nor has his allegiance to the Jehovah's Witnesses. His team mates firmly believed he would be back within a year. I expected him to tire of his new-found devotions and get back in training the following season. So did Bill McGarry, who realised that an asset of at least £100,000 (his valuation at the time) would otherwise be lost. When he declared his interest in the movement no one at the ground took him seriously. The fact that he was taking himself so seriously only encouraged a great deal of mickey-taking. It was incredible to most of us that he should have drifted into religion. He seemed to me to be the last sort of person who would do so. And yet, on reflection, one could find plenty of precedents among gad-about youths who like to be seen around town in the smart places, lounging against their sports cars, conscious of their charisma, only to turn against it all and embrace the Bible. If there was a road to Damascus through Wolverhampton, Peter evidently stumbled on it and emerged as a single-minded convert. I did most of the tormenting and teasing to get him out of it, but in the end I had to confess defeat.

He did not take lightly the dressing-room jokes and would turn away in a huff. After he had announced his conversion people sent to him many books about Billy Graham and other revivalists. He was deeply immersed in a particular interpretation of the Bible, but was not yet able to make a reasonable, articulate case for it, to impress on us that he was being rational or sensible.

But for a chance call by a Jehovah's Witness at his house, he might have gone on to become one of the most brilliant footballers in the game and one of the game's highest paid stars. Next to George Best, he could well have been the biggest name in English football, combining looks with exceptional talent, before the arrival on the football scene of Trevor Francis and Kevin Keegan.

It is regrettable that those already inside the faith and practising it did not try to persuade him to stay in football. I'm sure no one put pressure on him to give up, but I did not hear of anyone in the movement assuring him that he could best serve his faith by playing the game according to the rules he alleged were being bent and twisted by cloggers. He resented being idolised by the crowds – an overseer of his faith, whom he invited to see an evening match, shocked him by saying that on the pitch he resembled a Roman gladiator wanting the acclaim of the crowd.

The irony is that Peter Knowles, for all his protestations about the state of the game and its fierce competitiveness, lacked moral courage on the pitch. How could he possibly have been afraid he might inflict injury on an opponent when some of his temperamental outbursts were limited to kicking the ball away (on one occasion out of the ground) and to arguing with referees? Time and again I saw him pull out of tackles against rugged defenders. His tantrums never suggested that he could become involved in hard, physical play. Was it that, a fear of getting hurt as the game became more competitive, which influenced his decision to give up his career when it was moving in top gear? Was it failure of nerve at a decisive point in his career? They are difficult questions to answer because he has not been forthcoming. All he has said is that he made the right decision, that he has no regrets. Cleaning windows, which is what he does now (a symbol of his need to clean away his past and see into his future?) makes a sharp contrast with what he could be doing in league and international football, but he maintains he has found peace and contentment, which he could not have found inside the game. I really hope he has.

I suspect that his temperament was the real reason for his defection and religious conversion was the 'occasion' for giving up a lucrative and conspicuous career. We all look for something to cling to and Peter Knowles found it in religion, or a particular version of it. I do not want to argue the issue, but I believe he made a wrong decision at a critical time of his life. He allowed his conviction to get the better of his judgment. An incident in America convinced me that the 'newfound enlightenment' was arrogance.

I had been involved in the home championship at the end of the 1968–9 season and I did not want to go back to America, as I had been there in 1967 and grown tired of the razmataz associated with soccer. But I was directed, in no uncertain terms by Bill McGarry to be there and I flew into Atlanta two weeks behind the rest of the players.

From the airport I was given a lift by Eric Woodward, Aston Villa's Commercial Manager, to a hotel where I was not booked in and if it hadn't been for the non-appearance of Harry Parkes at that time a director of Aston Villa, I wouldn't have had a room for the night. So much for American efficiency.

It was when I arrived in Kansas where the Wolves were based that I experienced a Peter Knowles tantrum, linked with his religious persuasion. Before the start of a match it was customary to stand for the two national anthems. Peter remained seated on the bench and this rankled me. I asked my team mates how long this had been going on and they said, 'Since we arrived here to play.' I called to Bill McGarry to get him to stand, but he didn't or couldn't. A little of my respect for both of them died out there. So much for McGarry's authority.

83

Whatever his religious convictions, Peter should have stood for the National Anthem, just as I have seen Roman Catholics in the Northern Ireland team stand with Protestants for the National Anthem before a game even though they might have felt a closer affinity with the Catholic anthem of Southern Ireland. Irish Catholics can be just as devoted to the Mother Country as Protestants.

Peter Knowles professed to have found faith outside the game and to have lost it within the game. I wonder if he was aware that a vital spark was missing from his game. There was the natural ability and effortless power, as when he would draw back either foot half a yard and strike the ball fifty or sixty yards without even a run-up. Few footballers could do that, with such grace and style. But as a footballer he did not believe in himself. He lacked true grit.

There was a lot of mourning by young fans when Peter played his final game at Molineux on 6 September 1969 against Nottingham Forest. We drew 3–3 and I was among the scorers. The walls outside the ground were plastered with messages, urging him to stay. Girls were in tears and the crowd chanted: 'Peter, please don't go,' and 'Peter, we love you.' He seemed unmoved. To this day many supporters have not forgotten him and some have not forgiven him, because he deprived them of the thrill of his talent. How much a talented player owes to himself and how much to his supporters, is debatable. Peter didn't debate it. He took off his boots and went, never to return; not even in testimonial games apart from one for his brother Cyril, at Spurs. He has been asked many times to play in testimonials at Molineux for his former colleagues and he has always refused.

Danny Hegan was a bigger loss than Peter Knowles. Danny was more fun. His jokes lowered the tension and boosted morale enormously when results were not going our way and Bill McGarry was bearing down on us. Hugh Curran was another good humorist who knew how to raise a laugh at the right psychological time, to lift the dressing-room spirits. And they did need raising, on numerous occasions, especially when we were doing our best and getting no praise from the manager or much encouragement.

Footballers are sensitive souls. They may not give this impression, but I've not known any who do not need encouragement and who have failed to respond to praise when it is due.

In our first venture into European competition in the 1971–2 season I managed to score decisive goals which helped us to win through to the final of the UEFA Cup.

It was an exciting time, particularly as we had visions of emulating Wolves of the fifties and doing competitively in Europe what our forerunners had done on a friendly basis. In a league match four days before our UEFA fixture against Academica Coimbra in Portugal on 30 September I scored a hat-trick against Nottingham Forest. I went on to cap this with another hat-trick in Portugal and I was later told by colleagues on the bench that my third goal in this game had Bill McGarry jumping in the air. A long kick by Phil Parkes on a wet and windy night was carried down the pitch and bounced just outside their penalty box. Two of the opposing defenders went with me for the ball as it came dropping out of the dark sky. At the last moment I checked out, they kept running and jumped together, colliding with each other. Both missed the ball and as they lay in a tangle I hit the ball with all the force I could muster. I never saw it beat the goalkeeper. I knew it was on its way into the net, when I turned to receive the acclaim of my team mates. I had not scored another goal quite like it in my career. It was one of those shots you know is goal-bound the moment it leaves your foot.

And yet, afterwards, there was no word of compliment from Bill McGarry; not a single word. Surely, our first hat-trick in Europe justified at least a comment or passing remark.

If he felt that a few words of praise would have made me big-headed I could have informed him that this would have been better than the depression his silence caused. Could he really be so deprived of emotion that he could fail to display any feeling of delight when we came off the pitch? Was there really no word of congratulation that could have formed on his lips when we returned to Molineux? I thought about it and felt confirmed in my view that we were living in an open prison. Molineux from the outside looked just as it had in the glory days of the fifties. Inside the atmosphere was strained and far from cordial. I would arrive home from training and say to my wife, 'You'd never believe what's happened now. We've been told not to laugh or joke while we're training. We've been told to keep all the jokes until after training.'

Only the calming influence of my wife prevented me from exploding with rage. I needed her ability to lower my temperature even more after I had been injured in collision with Everton's Keith Newton at Goodison Park, in January 1970. It was by far the worst injury I suffered in my playing football. Phil Parkes kicked one of his usual long high balls. It was veering towards the right and I could see Bertie Lutton, playing at outside right, waiting for me to flick it on towards him. I leapt for the ball and as I turned my head, as I had done many times before, to guide the ball, I failed to see Keith Newton until it was too late. I hit the back of his head. My injuries were so severe that the Everton club doctor wanted me admitted to hospital in Liverpool. I preferred to travel back to Wolverhampton in the players' coach and get attention closer to home. I also thought of the inconvenience to my family if they had to travel to Liverpool to visit me.

On the way back down the motorway Bill McGarry did not speak to me or come to my seat to see how I was. When we reached Molineux his only concern was to get the Saturday sports papers from a groundsman, as he always did on returning from an away game.

What had I done to deserve this long silence on the journey? I had gone for the ball and come off badly, with my face broken in four places, which meant I would have to go to hospital for an extensive operation.

In a private hospital X-rays showed I would need a major operation. Doctors and surgeons gathered round me and I was told I would have to spend at least three weeks in hospital. Thirty stitches were needed in the side of my head, under my left eye and in my mouth. They had to go through my mouth to wire the bone which had broken under my left eye. Catching sight of my face in a mirror, I was horrified. I looked grotesque. But the physical pain could not compare with the deepest pain inside.

There were no strict visiting hours. I was in a private ward by myself and anyone from the club could call whenever it was convenient for them. A number of the players called to see how I was, but there was no visitor from the managerial staff. Bill

McGarry never came to see me, nor was there any message from him. The club sent a basket of fruit, which was common practice when a player entered hospital. The club chairman, John Ireland, and the assistant secretary, Jack Robinson, asked after me, but one expects in these circumstances personal contact from one's own manager or his training staff.

If I had been a manager and one of my players had been injured and put into hospital I would have been there that night or the next day, at his bedside.

I felt I had given Wolves enough service to justify at least a message of sympathy or a get-well card from the manager, but there was not one among the piles of letters and cards I received from supporters and football fans throughout the country, including many Evertonians.

This apparent indifference depressed me, because it made me feel I was not officially wanted at Molineux and the administration did not care about my being laid up and out of the game for weeks or months.

Lying there not even able to pick at the grapes and flicking through magazines and books I told my wife: 'If you don't get me out of here I shall jump out of the window.' After ten days I discharged myself and went home to complete my convalescence. The doctors, who were dubious about letting me leave, assured me that I would not be able to play again until the following season. That meant eight months on the sidelines, more than my patience could stand. I had proved doctors wrong in the past. In 1961, after a car crash which left me with a broken arm and head and face wounds needing fifty stitches, I had returned within three months after being ruled out for six months. I could prove them wrong again.

On other occasions I simply had to overcome physical setbacks. This time my moral was low. As chairman of the local branch of the Mental Health Research Fund, I knew how a problem on the mind can be even more unsettling and harder to cope with, than a broken leg or cheek-bone. Not surprisingly, 50 per cent of the country's hospital beds are occupied by patients with mental problems.

My recovery would have been eased if the club, represented by Bill McGarry, had taken some interest in what was happening

87

to me. It was not just a matter of recovering from my injuries and reclaiming my position in the side; it was trying to convince myself, against the evidence, that I was not really wanted by McGarry and that until he was forced to acknowledge my return, he was shutting me out of his mind. That is how it seemed to me. Insult had been added to injury.

For the next two months, during my recovery, I tried to busy myself at home and did not go near the ground. I waited in vain for a phone call from Molineux. No one rang to inquire about me. I was a forgotten man. This may seem incredible but this is how it was.

One lunch time, over two months later, when I was feeling much better I decided to take my wife out to lunch and we called at a pub in Wolverhampton run by a good pal, Bill Hancock, who has been a Wolves supporter for many years and liked to talk about football. When I was in hospital after injury resulting from the car crash in 1961 during my Aston Villa days Bill brought in my food all prepared with meat chopped into small pieces as I had broken my left arm, my good arm, and had only one hand free. As Jutta and I walked in, on our way to the grill room, who should be coming out but Bill McGarry, accompanied by Hugh Jamieson, a journalist from Sheffield who had just come down to the Midlands to represent *The Sun* newspaper. To say the least, it was embarrassing for him. My immediate instinct, as we approached, was to let fly, and not only with a few well-chosen words. I'll never know how I restrained myself from striking him. My wife sensed what was going through my mind and said quietly: 'Keep your head. Don't say or do anything you'll regret.' I really wish I had hit him whatever the consequences.

Bill McGarry had a habit when talking to me of keeping his gaze fixed towards the floor. I can only remember him ever looking at me directly a few times and this wasn't one of them. As we met at the pub entrance he said, 'How are you?' looking down at my feet. I should have said: 'They're all right,' meaning my feet, which he appeared to be addressing. I said: 'I'm a little better, thank you.' That was all. End of conversation.

He did not ask when I expected to be back in training or what the doctors had told me. Just a casual 'How are you?'

Practising taking corner kicks during training

I'm still proud to have played for Aston Villa

Obeying the MEB instruction

Playing against Liverpool at Molineux

Wearing 'Irish' shirts in Los Angeles

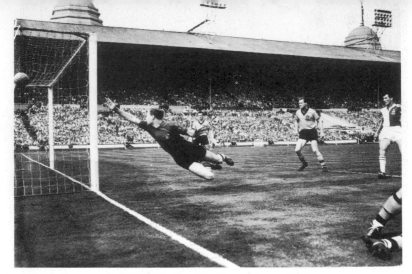

At Wembley for Blackburn Rovers 1960

Who said Football was a serious game?

In serious mood during Freedom of Contract negotiations

Asa Hartford showing the only way to contain David Wagstaffe

Seven against one is just not fair – even the linesman cannot bear to watch

Spot the odd man out in this line up at St James's Park, Newcastle

In action against West Ham at Molineux

Could be a spot the ball competition

Appreciating John Osborne of West Bromwich – a much underrated English goalkeeper

Peter Knowles got as much satisfaction as I did after I opened the scoring against Southampton at Molineux

Doing the trainer's job ...

Action suspended — for two months

The old man of the sea

Wolves' lucky boat came in two days later at Wembley, winning the League Cup Final against Manchester City

*No, not Butch Cassidy and the Sundance Kid – but John Richards and I
as sharpshooters on and off the pitch*

Final league match against Leeds at Molineux

'Thanks for the Memory' Bill – and I'm not referring to Billy Bremner

No difficulty in guessing who scored

The King (Denis Law) and I

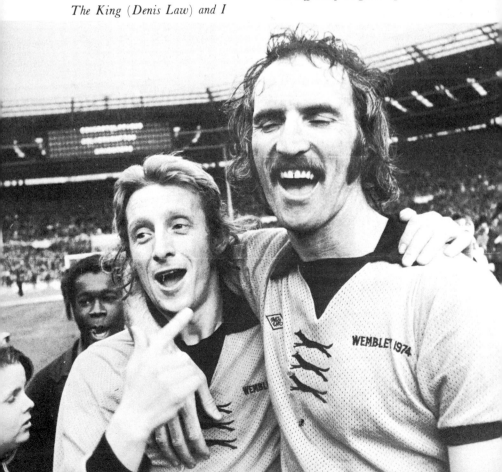

In days before advertising was fashionable on shirt fronts

The many faces of yours truly

that did not even carry with it the anxiousness of a manager who was without his leading goalscorer. This brief encounter after more than two months, on the doorstep of a pub, destroyed my appetite for lunch. I sat at a table wondering if he was peering from behind the door to make sure I did not order a prawn cocktail!

This had become a club joke, but a sour one. Not long after he had taken over at Wolves, we had a cup-tie at Hull. A few days were spent at Southport in training and on the Friday we made our way to Hull where we were booked into a hotel for the night. In the evening we went into the hotel restaurant for dinner and John Holsgrove, the Wolves no. 6 at the time, ordered a prawn cocktail. Bill McGarry heard him. If Holsey had ordered a blow-out of champagne, roast turkey and plum duff there could not have been more consternation.

'What do you think this is?' he shouted. 'Butlins holiday camp?' Holsey was flabbergasted. All he had done was ask for a prawn cocktail. What was wrong with that? Everything, according to Bill McGarry, who made it known that prawn cocktails were bad for footballers and he would not allow any Wolves player to eat one when he was around. It often occurred to me if he worried how many prawn cocktails they ate when he was not around, tucking into them at home.

He was fastidious about the diet of his players. At lunch he would not allow anyone to have more than one bread roll. Two bread rolls meant breaking the carbohydrate barrier and he would not stand for that. When a waiter brought extra bread rolls I thought McGarry would have a fit; what a fuss, I thought, about bread rolls. He seemed to be obsessed by them. Another one of his quirks was his refusal to allow us to have a cup of tea in hotels unless we paid for it. This had less to do with tannic acid than the cost, which also explained why we were not allowed to make telephone calls from hotel bedrooms at the club's expense. These were little things we had enjoyed as a matter of course before he came; small 'perks' most big clubs accept automatically. As Bill McGarry came from a more cost-conscious section of the league his thriftiness must have been second nature. I still wonder to this day if he paid for his own tea and hotel telephone calls.

I had not come across this kind of managerial attitude before in my career, except under Freddie Cox at Portsmouth in 1958. Freddie had practically counted the chips on a player's plate!

When Bill McGarry blew up over prawn cocktails and bread rolls he was treating us as children – but oddly enough I have never liked prawn cocktails. It was not so much the dietary restriction that irked us as the way of imposing it. If he had civilly explained to us his view of what was good and bad to eat at lunch before a game, there would have been no attempts to 'get even' behind his back. Another item on the black list was sweets, except for barley sugar, which he considered energising. This did not mean players going without their sweets. At motorway cafés or wherever we stopped on journeys, one player would keep a look-out while another dashed to a shop to buy them. The young players would eat the sweets secretively at the back of the coach. Bill McGarry usually sat near the front and did not know what rebellious munching was going on behind him! But there was nothing we could do on the coach to make up for the apple pie and trifle he refused to let the players have for dessert, allowing only ice-cream or cheese and biscuits in hotels or restaurants.

Some of the players lightened their moods over these petty restrictions by imagining what they would do if they won the pools, and one of the most popular anticipated pleasures was to order a lunch of prawn cocktails, apple pie and trifle, known as the Bill McGarry Special!

Some ten years after John Holsgrove had discovered that prawn cocktails were 'off the menu', I happened to run into Tommy Craig and his wife at Aston Villa, on his arrival from Newcastle. 'How were things up there?' I asked. 'How did you get on with Bill McGarry?' I thought I detected a pained expression on his face, but he did not say much until I asked him if he had experienced McGarry's attitude towards players' eating habits.

'Funny you should mention that,' he said, telling me of a Newcastle player who was sitting down to a prawn cocktail when McGarry came from behind and snatched it away from him, on the grounds that prawn cocktails were not good for players before a match. The player said, 'He had been eating them for five years without their doing him any harm.'

Not long afterwards I met up with another Newcastle player

and he asked me how I had put up with the McGarry style of management for seven years. I could only reply: 'I really don't know' – and to this day, the more I think about it, I still don't know (I won't accept the argument that I must have been a masochist!).

The barrier between McGarry and me seemed to be electrified and he controlled the current. On a few occasions he switched off, so that I was able to cross over and speak to him on almost equal, man-to-man terms, but there was never much response. I could have understood his attitude towards me if I had been late for training, which I never was; if I missed the coach or train, which I never did; if I had said or written anything to the detriment of the club, which I never did. After a while I felt that he thought I was after his job. Various people, inside and outside the club, told me that he was convinced of this. The idea had never crossed my mind. With hindsight, he should now realise I was not after his job.

Most managers like to keep tabs on their players at all times, on and off the pitch. I had the impression that Bill McGarry was suspicious of me because he never knew what I was doing away from the ground and could not tie me down. Nor could he replace me in the side but, oh, how he tried. Time and again he sought and sometimes bought players who were intended to oust me from the forward line. I know this because the players who came told me so. This only acted as a supercharger, making me more determined than ever to hold my place and put paid to his efforts.

I sympathised with my potential replacements because it meant an extra burden for them to carry in the attack. They knew that only by scoring more goals and playing better could they fulfil the purpose for which they had been signed.

Among those who at various times had the job of trying to edge me out of the attack were Hugh Curran, Bobby Gould and Steve Kindon. Alan Sunderland was also tried at centre forward. None of these manoeuvres worked the way Bill McGarry hoped and eventually I struck a formidable goal-scoring partnership with John Richards. Only one factor marred our memorable partnership – the age difference. He was a young player on his way up and I was over the thirty mark, when every season enlarges the question-mark against your

91

name and the last lap is coming nearer. If I had been ten years younger, we would have set post-war records that no partnership would have equalled in the first division.

Before our partnership developed and we were taking the first division in our stride, the aggravations at Molineux had become almost unbearable and I seriously began to consider pulling out of the game. It was absurd to sit on the coach for anything up to six or seven hours without a word passing between me and the manager, sitting four feet away. The sullen silence was portentous and it nagged me into testing his opinion of me. On a club tour of Sweden, in the pre-season, of July 1971 I asked myself whether I needed all this nonsense, the irksome restrictions and the constant feeling that I had done something to incur McGarry's disapproval. More than three years had gone by with McGarry in charge and I was no nearer to a mutual understanding. If anything, we were further apart than on the day he arrived. I was beginning to feel like one of Kafka's characters, wondering if I was the guilty party, guilty of some unspecified crime.

Two years before he had prevented my joining Arsenal. Although I had gone on record at Wolves saying that I wanted to finish my playing career at Molineux, that was under Ronnie Allen. An opportunity of joining Arsenal in the summer of 1969 came about through Gordon Clark, who had been my manager at Peterborough, where he had declared that if I left he would go too (could a player ask for more loyalty than that from his manager?). Now, four years later, he was chief scout with Arsenal and began the moves to get me. The prospect of going to Highbury excited me and I would have been even more excited had I imagined that within two years Arsenal would become the second club this century to win the double.

Obviously, McGarry did not want me and he was looking for a replacement. Why then didn't the deal go through? I was never told, but Arsenal were higher in the first division than Wolves and I wondered if the position of the two clubs influenced his refusal to let me go. If Arsenal had been struggling near the bottom, would he have agreed? I can only speculate. In my opinion, it all amounted to bad faith and an antipathy between us. Generally managers are loath to let players go to better clubs.

To return to the Stanley Rous tournament in Sweden – I told him I wanted to have a chat with him and said I was thinking of retiring at the end of the season. His only response was: 'I can get a lot of money for you.' That was all. To a degree, I was only bluffing, to test his reaction. I knew now that I was only an object, or some sort of merchandise with a price tag. This is why I have been obsessed with the need to change the system which puts an unnatural distance between player and manager. Between McGarry and me the air was cleared for a while and the tension eased just a little. We decided to carry on and take each season as it came. As long as I was scoring goals – averaging over fifteen a season in all competitions, and what manager would baulk a player who could guarantee that? – I knew I could keep my position in the side on merit.

Seven

As the former chairman of the Professional Footballers' Association, I have persisted with moves to introduce a form of freedom of contract, because it would give players firmer rights and greater degrees of independence. They would have more say in their own careers, as do people in other trades and professions. The system we have accepted for far too long treats players as serfs, reducing them to the cattle market, where they are bought and sold, and at their clubs kept in line by the powers-that-be. These powers are extremely autocratic. Managers can deprive players of large amounts of money, fining them two weeks' salary for flimsy reasons. It is money most players can ill afford to lose and such fines rarely achieve their objects, unless the object is to demonstrate a manager's hold over a player. What other trade or profession would accept so casually the disciplinary measures often imposed by clubs on top of disciplinary penalties imposed by the football authorities? Double punishments are commonplace. Players are systematically 'enslaved' and few are willing, except through their union, to challenge the despotic rule.

The law as it has been for generations, is on the side of the big battalions, led by boards of directors and managers. This is gradually changing, but not many players would take it on themselves to appeal to the Football Association over internal discipline imposed by their managers. They know their lives would become unbearable in future, so they buckle down and take what comes, thinking of their mortgage commitments, their families and their team places. As a committee member, then as chairman of the PFA, I helped Bill McGarry to sort out a number of problems involving players' contracts but this did not precipitate a better understanding between us. I did my best to settle disputes, acting as arbiter, because I appreciated the importance of morale. When players are dissatisfied over their conditions their minds are taken off the game and teamwork suffers. My own 'dispute' was not one that could be put right by negotiation, because it amounted to a clash of personalities.

Friction and clashes often occur between managers and players but do not always get into the press. They are regarded as 'domestic matters', but are in fact professional issues and should be treated as such. The system is at fault for creating the conditions that allow grown men to be treated as irresponsible boys. It has become difficult for many people, inside and outside the game, to think of footballers as men. They are 'the lads' or 'the boys'.

My position with the PFA and my seniority in age made no difference to my standing at Molineux where I felt, many times, that I was being treated like a child.

Two days before the start of the 1973-4 season an incident occurred which gave me a choice between obeying an instruction and quitting the club rather than pay a fine, which would have been my second time in twenty-five years. Not the record of a rebel! It would, in fact, have been my first genuine fine in my career and I wanted to keep my record clean. Our pre-season training programme was based on all-out effort. We exerted every muscle, we ran, we jumped, we did all the exercises in the book and more besides. No team in the country, in Europe even, could have been fitter for the start of the season. Two days before the opening match against Norwich I was scheduled to appear at a local store as part of a promotional campaign. It was a personal commercial engagement I had accepted because it was timed for a Thursday afternoon which was free time. I had never missed a training session for any commercial reason. My appearance at the store was advertised in the local press on Wednesday evening. At lunchtime on Thursday, after we had finished normal training the coach, Sammy Chung, told us we had to report back in the afternoon for further training. Senior players never reported back on Thursday afternoon unless they were recovering from injury. When I asked why, he explained: 'We're coming back for some sprinting.' This had never happened before in my time at Molineux and it struck me as odd. I have never trained on a Thursday, before or after that incident.

95

What was I to do about it? There was no time to rearrange the store promotion. If I did not turn up the organisers, who had gone to some expense in their advertising, would be left to apologise to people on my behalf and there would be cynical response from customers, thinking they had been 'conned'. On the other hand, if I failed to turn up for afternoon training I knew I would be disciplined by the manager and fined.

In the circumstances, I decided to ignore the extra training session and fulfil my obligations at the store. Afterwards, I had another decision to make. Should I go meekly to the ground and accept my inevitable punishment or say, 'To hell with it ... I'm clearing out?' I pondered the question for a while, then picked up the phone at home and called the assistant secretary, Jack Robinson. 'Hello, Jack,' I said. 'Do something for me, will you? Sort out my insurance cards and have them ready for me to collect. I'll be in in the morning to pick them up.' When he asked why I wanted them, I said: 'I've finished with Bill McGarry, Jack.'

I was putting myself in an ambiguous position. Part of me wanted to get away and another part clung to Wolves. I was determined to quit rather than be humiliated by a fine, and I was part bluffing. I knew that Jack would have to go to Bill McGarry and tell him what I was doing, as this was his job.

The moment I arrived at the ground on the Friday morning I asked Jack Dowen, who looked after the kit, to put my two pairs of boots into a plastic bag. Next, I went to the dressing room to collect my mail and say cheerio to the players. Because we had been forbidden to enter the general office, the mail had to be brought to the dressing room and left for us. I was leaving a trail and knew that alarm signals were reaching the manager's office.

After a few minutes Sammy Chung came into the dressing room to tell me that the manager wanted to see me in his office. Tucking my boots under my arm, I tapped on the door and waited for him to call me in. 'What's your problem?' he asked, sitting behind his desk. I was not in the mood to catalogue my grievances. I said: 'It's incredible what you did yesterday.' He looked up at me – one of the rare times he did – looked surprised and asked what I meant. I told him. 'Having the players back in the afternoon ... I wouldn't have accepted that promotion

96

job if I thought we'd be training again. I find it odd, that's all.' He pleaded innocence and assured me that it had nothing to do with my advertised engagement. But the coincidence was too great for me to give him the benefit of the doubt.

If I had run foul of a normal training session, why was I not disciplined? I left his office without a fine and I thought it best not to tell my colleagues of this. Some of them had been fined just for being late for training on occasions and I knew they would not take kindly to my being 'let off'.

I went straight to the dressing room and murmured quietly to David Wagstaffe, who had his own problems at the club and was not always treated too well, that I must have set a record for the shortest retirement in the history of the game – twenty minutes! Waggy, who was vastly underrated by the manager and coach, at one stage also asked for his cards and walked out for a few days. There was a tremendous bond between us. In the dressing room we often exchanged mutual grievances and niggles with each other.

If Bill McGarry had disciplined me with a fine I would have quit Wolves there and then.

Nothing more was said and the next day, the opening match of the season, I scored two of our goals in a 3–1 defeat of Norwich. Being absent without leave on Thursday afternoon had not affected my goal-scoring abilities. In spite of this encouraging start to the playing season, problems weighed heavily on my mind. I tried to shake them off by getting stuck into the action on the pitch and I scored in all the opening five games in the league. While the goals came my way, they eluded my partner, John Richards, for the first time. He was going through one of those dark patches that come the way of most footballers from time to time. He tried not to show it, but he was worried. The harder he tried, the more difficult it became. His anxiety was upsetting his play and his confidence was ebbing. In the two previous seasons he had scored most of our goals in our partnership and now he could not understand why everything was going wrong for him. He was fit and fast, but the goals just would not come.

His morale was not helped by rumours appearing in the national sports pages that he might be left out of our UEFA fixture in Portugal on 26 September 1973 against Bellenges,

John was going through a period when he needed special encouragement and reassurance which should have come from the manager. Lots of strikers go through lean periods and usually emerge to get back into their stride. I remembered a similar goal famine when I was with Leicester, and how I had to sort myself out, with no help from Matt Gillies. John was in a similar position and was no longer confident of his place in the side.

Something had to be done and I took it on myself to bring home the message to Bill McGarry. But how? I wanted to walk straight up to him and say: 'Now look here. You're not treating young John Richards right. Why don't you tell him not to worry, just to get on with the game and assure him the goals will come ...' I was rehearsing in my mind what to say when I came down to breakfast in our hotel the morning of the match.

My room mate, Gerry Taylor, had gone down to the breakfast room and was sitting at a table with McGarry. There were two vacant places, but I walked past and took a seat at a table by myself. The gesture did not pass unnoticed. After breakfast Sammy Chung said 'the boss' wanted to see me in his hotel room.

If there was to be a confrontation I knew exactly what I was going to say. McGarry asked why I had sat by myself. I had been intentionally unfriendly and he had sensed it. I wasn't going to beat about the breakfast table: 'I don't agree with the way you are treating John Richards,' I said. 'His confidence is sagging and I'm doing my best to keep him going. If he's out, it will affect me. Instead of the goals being shared I'm lucky, I'm getting them at the moment. But it could easily be the other way round. You're taking it out on him so I'm taking it out on you. He's no bother to you. He's too nice a kid to be treated like this. He's never given you a problem on or off the pitch all the time he's been at the club.'

I hadn't said so much to him for a long time. Normally our conversations were brief, usually terse. The words came gushing out because I was furious. 'He's a hell of a trainer,' I went on. 'And he's dedicated.' I didn't want it to sound like a testimonial, but it was time to remind him exactly what John Richards meant to the side and to me. Our partnership on the pitch had developed a great bond between us.

I knew what McGarry had in mind and why he was allowing

John to remain in doubt about his striking role. He thought that if the player got the backlash in the press and was put on a spot about his lack of goals, he would be more determined than ever to break the hoodoo. This tactic may work with some players. John was not being stimulated by what seemed to be a down on him. He was more depressed and felt insecure.

I don't know whether my remarks carried weight with Bill McGarry or if he had already made up his mind, but John was in the team that night. I recalled how I had pleaded for Danny Hegan not to be dropped when he was going through a critical period, pointing out that to leave him out would have ruined him.

The game in Portugal had not long been underway when it happened. John scored the opening goal. I shall never forget the look of relief on his face and reaction on the pitch after sticking it away, nor the jubilation of his team mates as they threw themselves over him in delight. His relief was theirs too. The number one scorer in the English League was back on scoring form and this affected the entire team.

Strangely, or so it seemed at the time, in the second half he did something completely out of character and against the standards he had set for himself. He got involved in a nasty incident and struck an opponent and he was sent off. Thinking about it afterwards I realised that this was the result of pent-up emotions being released, not an act of malice. Tensions can do odd things to players, causing them to behave in uncharacteristic ways on the spur of a moment. It was the speculation about his position in the side which had troubled him and shaken his composure. When players are sometimes seen in flare-ups on the pitch and when they react violently to provocation, it is assumed they are behaving like hooligans. The truth is that their aggression might have little or nothing to do with the incidents in which they are involved and that these incidents trigger-off explosive forces that have been held down for some time, originating off the pitch.

Apart from one incident John Richards was himself again, and the game went our way. David Wagstaffe, a winger who never received his proper recognition, at international level, chiefly because of Alf Ramsey's World Cup omission of traditional wingers who were promptly put out of fashion in the league – hit a cross and I was on the other end to head the ball into the net. We won 2–0.

John and I re-affirmed our scoring partnership which ran for over three years. My lasting regret is that we did not have more seasons together. We complemented each other perfectly. I could win the ball in the air, nod it down and he knew how to crack it in. Or I would send him away towards goal with a through pass . . . Time and again we split defences with simple, one-two movements and scored goals from 'impossible' situations. It was a lethal partnership, aided and abetted by the wing service of David Wagstaffe.

Taken at the flood of goals, we could have gone on to fortune. Wolves were capable of winning the championship, the FA Cup and other honours. But for Pat Jennings in the Spurs goal, proving himself the best goalkeeper in the world at the time, we would have won the UEFA Cup instead of losing in the final. The difference between Spurs and Wolves in the 1972 League Cup semi-final was Pat Jennings. One man does not make a team, but a world-class goalkeeper can seal the success of a good side which is what Peter Shilton has done for Brian Clough's Nottingham Forest, and Ray Clemence for Liverpool.

It was by no means a new experience for me to be in a side whose full potential was not grasped at the vital moment. At Blackburn I was in a forward line-up with Bryan Douglas, Peter Dobing, Roy Vernon and Ally McLeod (the former Scotland manager), possibly the most complete forward line in the history of Blackburn Rovers.

Sometimes a player can see this and a manager cannot. At other times a manager can see it but cannot impress the fact on his players. My fate seemed to be in forward lines and teams that were broken up through lack of managerial foresight or players not having enough confidence in their own ability.

At Wolves, I firmly believed it was lack of positive encouragement and tensions caused by backstage pettiness that prevented the side from living up to the glory days of the fifties. We would joke about some of the ludicrous situations and trivial arguments that went on behind the scenes, but this was just a way of compensating for pressures that should never have been put on us. For instance, not long after I had returned to the first team after my facial injury we played Burnley, a sorrowful side

100

that appeared capable of first division thrust but never quite clicked. It was the last game of the season and a few minutes from time I met a corner with my head and the ball went like a sputnik into the back of the net to win the game 1–0. That should have pleased McGarry, but he was more concerned about our overall performance, as we discovered afterwards in the dressing room.

Since coming to the Midlands in 1961 I was surprised by a regional taste for sterilised milk, which I cannot drink. In my tea I always have pasteurised milk. At Molineux the tea was always served with sterilised milk and at half-time, when tea for the players was brought into the dressing room, I preferred to go without. After a match, I would go to the tea-room, close to the dressing room, where the tea ladies gave me tea with pasteurised milk or I would ask one of the apprentices to fetch me a cup.

Since I signed on 16 March 1967 this had been the practice and when Bill McGarry arrived he paid no attention to it – until after the Burnley match. He was in the dressing room, moaning and groaning about our performance, when Jack Davis, a pensioner who had at one time been first-team trainer and connected with Wolves for over half a century, came in with my cup of tea.

McGarry glowered and shouted: 'Get that ... tea out of here!' If the tea the rest of the players was drinking was not good enough, he went on, then ... The rest of his words were lost in mutterings, as he gave us a verbal lashing.

I felt sorry for the old fellow who had walked right into it. It was too much. I had to say something. 'Why are you taking it out on the old boy? I've been having a cup of tea with pasteurised milk all the time I've been here.' All he said in reply was: 'If it's good enough for me to drink, it's good enough for you.'

In the showers the players didn't talk about the game or our performance, all they talked about was my cup of tea. 'Hey Doog, why didn't you tell him to f... off?' one of them said. 'Why didn't *you*?' I asked and he replied, 'You must be kidding.' I could not let the matter rest there. It was too ridiculous and I was steaming when I came out of the showers, ready for a confrontation. I dressed and went to his office, banging on

101

the door. When I went in he held up his hands. 'All right,' he said. 'I was out of order, I was wrong. I was wild with my defence for letting them through so many times ...'

(Actually, it was Steve Kindon who broke through the defence so many times. I am convinced he was signed by McGarry on the strength of this performance, to replace me.)

'It had nothing to do with old Mr Davis,' I said. 'That sort of scene isn't any good for morale.'

I found that if one challenged Bill McGarry there was a good chance of him backing down. But it wasn't always possible or advisable to do this. Sometimes a little stealth or cunning were preferable. I used this tactic in another niggle in European competitions when, with fifteen players in the squad, he refused to pay the full bonus to the players who were not used. This did not make sense to the players. If fifteen were chosen, why not pay them all the same bonus? There was no point in arguing about it, but there was something I could do about it eventually. The rule provided that if two substitutes were used, the other two not used had to get the full bonus. To make sure that two substitutes came on, I suggested that if we had a commanding lead fifteen or so minutes from time, one or two of us would come off. It didn't always work out this way, of course. As I was the oldest it usually fell to me to come off and give a substitute the opportunity of guaranteeing the bonus for the full first-team squad. It was a matter of team spirit. It is a pity I had to resort to subterfuge to get what we should have been given, as a matter of principle.

There was nothing we could do though on the occasion when Hugh Curran failed to join the Wolves coach on time as it left White Hart Lane after the match against Spurs in the UEFA Cup Final on Wednesday, 17 May 1972. No one at first noticed that he was not on the coach. Twenty minutes later someone said: 'We've left Hughie behind!' Sid Kipping, our coach driver, was about to turn back but McGarry instructed him to keep going, leaving Hughie to make his own way back to Wolverhampton. That was another example of the famed McGarry discipline, insistence on punctuality – to the minute. For the record, Hughie Curran didn't take too kindly to this inconvenience.

It became increasingly hard, over the years, to accept these

102

idiosyncrasies, pressures and restrictions without protest. When depression began to get the better of me, I would turn my thoughts to the town itself. Wolverhampton had become my home, not just because I happened to be making my living there, but because I had come to know the people and enjoy their friendliness.

I was made welcome wherever I went, the first time since leaving Ireland that I had truly felt at ease with my surroundings and with the people I met. There is tremendous generosity in the town, as I found in my fund-raising activities for the Mental Health Research Fund and at whatever charity functions I attended. I liked to be involved in the life of the town, which I felt was something which went against me with Bill McGarry. My photograph was often in the papers, at some social function or other, and I was often being invited to speak at Rotary clubs, schools, football forums and college societies; open fetes, present awards, attend dinners ... My wife often pleaded with me to turn down requests, as I would have been out every night to the neglect of my family. Throughout my career I have, at times, neglected my family because of the importance I have attached to my professional duties and responsibilities.

Footballers who enjoy a certain amount of popularity and a marked degree of success in their careers, owe something to their communities. Football does not exist in a social vacuum. It is entirely dependent on public response. Players have to respond too and not only on the pitch. They need to get out and about, making friendly contact with their supporters.

At Molineux, Bill McGarry never appeared to appreciate the value of public relations. He was not a public socialiser and rarely figured in public functions. He played squash, golf, and was often seen at these clubs, but otherwise he was not known personally about the town. He seemed to appear aloof, which did not endear him to the people of Wolverhampton and explains why so few objections were heard when he was given the sack.

He did not seem to understand that my social and professional activities off the pitch reflected my love of the club and the town. I wanted Wolves to be the best Midlands club in the League. My enthusiasm was interpreted as presumption, as on the occasions I pleaded with him to buy certain players,

103

such as Tommy McLean, Kilmarnock outside right who had played against us in America in June 1969. McLean was small but quick, an excellent passer of the ball. He could have joined Wolves, if an approach had been made, but went to Glasgow Rangers, where he has been a brilliant player for the past ten years, costing less than £100,000.

Another of my recommendations was, however, taken up – and then an opportunity tossed away.

In the summer of 1973 I went for six weeks to South Africa as a guest player with Arcadia Shepherds in Pretoria. A sturdy young centre forward, named Peter Withe, made an immediate impression on me. He had failed to get anywhere in the English League and after spells with Southport, Preston and Barrow had gone to South Africa to work as an electrician and play football as a part-time professional. I had never seen a player train harder or put more enthusiasm into his game. To me he had all the assets of a bustling and skilful centre forward and here he was, in Pretoria, going to waste.

When I returned I told Bill McGarry about him and suggested making an offer. Peter was brought over on a trial basis. He was nervous, anxious to make the right impression and quickly got down to the business of all-out training. He knew this was probably his last chance to make the grade in English League football. After ten weeks, McGarry sent for me and said: 'He's not going to make it. I shan't sign him.'

It was rough justice, I knew that he hadn't seen him in action, except for forty-five minutes in a reserve match at Sheffield. All I could say was: 'Well, I'm pleased you've given him an opportunity.'

I didn't tell Peter this. I just didn't have the heart. It was up to Bill McGarry to tell him and I could well imagine how despondent he would be, faced with the prospect of returning to South Africa and the obscurity of part-time football. Then fate intervened. In a Tuesday morning practice match – which Bill McGarry watched – the first team lost 4–0 to the reserves and Peter scored all four goals. It was like Roy of the Rovers. And to confirm it was no fluke, the next Saturday he scored a hat-trick in a West Midland league match. The following Saturday, in the reserves, he scored two more goals. Nine goals in three games.

104

McGarry had to reconsider his judgment. He sent for me again and this time he said: 'I think I'm going to sign him.' Arrangements were made with Arcadia to release him and he was bought for a pittance. He should have been put in a position to make full use of his talent. Instead, he was played out of position and his talent was squandered, until another club made a better assessment of it.

Peter liked the forward role, but was put in a supporting role and he could not fulfil his potential. When I suggested to Bill McGarry that he reverse the roles of John Richards and Peter, he said: 'No, it would never work.' He must have been wearing blinkers, for what he did with Peter Withe in the forward line never worked, at Wolves. Brian Clough soon recognised Peter's value after McGarry had sold him to Birmingham City, and at £50,000 he proved a valuable asset – in his proper position – at Nottingham Forest. At Wolves he did not have a fair chance, no doubt because I was involved. His talent was squandered and his opportunity was limited. It is incredible irony that after he had demonstrated his talent at Forest, McGarry should pay a reputed fee of £200,000 to take him to Newcastle.

Nor did a young player named John Rutter, who was denied the opportunity of making any headway when he was given a free transfer. At the end of a season the lad came to me, as the club's PFA representative, and told me what had happened. It seemed like the end of the world for him. In certain circumstances a free transfer can help a player to get settled quickly at another club with some financial advantage. It was not like that for John Rutter who had another year of his contract to run and felt he was being thrown out. I told him that 80 per cent of the boys who signed terms at seventeen were out of the game within five years. And I mentioned a number of great players who had been rejected and later made their names. It was one thing to talk to him consolingly in general terms, another to do something about his specific circumstances. When I heard that his contract had a year to go, I told him: 'They can't do that.'

I went to Bill McGarry and reminded him that a player's contract could not be broken in the middle of its course. He said he wasn't aware of the position. Perhaps not. The club secretary Phil Shaw should have been aware of it and informed the manager.

To legalise the situation, McGarry said he would not then give him a free transfer, but John was still unhappy. He said to me: 'How can I stay here when I'm not wanted?' I advised him not to act on impulse.

Time and again, at various, clubs, I had seen young players 'given the treatment' when they should have dug in and insisted on their rights. Some had been kept in the reserves or third team and left to rot, others had been told they would never kick a ball again. Pressure can be put on a player, even when he has all the legal rights on his side.

John eventually went to Bournemouth and then to Stockport. He deserved some success in the game. I admired his application. He was one of those young players who never gave any trouble, of good character, and all they ask is the opportunity to show what they can do.

In 1975 I too had a year to run in my contract, but before the end of the season I decided to retire. One reason was the recurrence of back trouble that had plagued me since my Aston Villa days. It prevented my going all out in training and weakened me when I needed all my strength and stamina. Another reason was weariness of spirit. For seven years I had devoted myself to Wolves under Bill McGarry's management without getting a word of thanks or encouragement. In eight and a half years at the club my salary had risen by only £20. My basic pay when I finished playing for Wolves was £100 a week, which I think shows that not all footballers are in the game just to make a fortune.

When I informed Bill McGarry of my decision my contract ran until 30 June 1976. After all my service to Wolves I was offered four weeks' wages. That was to be the pay-off. In McGarry's own words in his office: 'You can have a lump sum of four weeks' wages.' He knew I had the right to carry on for another year, which would have meant £6000 in basic salary.

'That's mean of you,' I said. I didn't want to argue about money, but I was not prepared to be shrugged off like that. Time and again in my years at Wolves I had scored winning goals. I had helped the side win promotion from the second division in my first season at Molineux and I think I had made

106

useful contributions. It was ironical, the way sports reporters had complimented him on half-time pep talks which had transformed the team in the second half, when all he had done was level a few expletives at us in the dressing room and winning goals in the second half had nothing to do with his instructions.

These thoughts went through my mind when I contemplated the final payment, four weeks' salary for eight years devotion, effort and application.

Strictly speaking I was entitled to £6000 when I left. A settlement was reached which gave me £1000. Later, when Bill McGarry was sacked after taking Wolves to the second division, they gave him almost £32,000 compensation for the breaking of his contract. The system favours managers above players, which is why I campaigned so hard, as chairman of the PFA, to introduce a form of freedom of contract that would enable players to get more equitable justice in the game and adequate rewards for their contributions.

I am all for a person getting what his ability warrants, but I am against others being denied equal rights.

It was a wrench leaving Molineux, but my departure could have been the highlight of my time there, had Bill McGarry not begrudged me the final limelight. My last season was full of ups and downs, mostly put-downs. Alan Sunderland, who replaced me, had been given the no. 10 shirt, unfortunately he broke a leg in training – for the record Alan went eighteen games without scoring and I had to be brought back, if only as a substitute. I came on for the injured Steve Kindon in one match and scored, our only goal at Middlesbrough. I was in the team, next week against Carlisle, who we beat 2–0, and I figured in a goalless draw at Everton, in the following league game. Three points out of four wasn't bad. But if I needed a reminder that I was still not in favour of permanent selection it came when we played in Portugal against Oporto on 18 September 1974. In the first half John McAlle played a long ball back from fifty yards. The ball went sailing over Phil Parkes's head, who was by this time on the eighteen yards line, and into the back of the net. The defence was letting in the goals, but at half-time I was taken off, McGarry said he had picked the wrong team, meaning that he should not have picked me. When we arrived back on Friday he said to me: 'You're not in the

107

squad tomorrow. You can either not play or play in the reserves.' As I had trained all week I decided that I might as well have a game and play in the reserves. The message was loud and clear. For as long as I stayed with Wolves, I would not be an automatic choice for the first team. For the first time in my career I would have to content myself with second team football unless injuries occurred and I was needed.

Then two weeks later on 2 October I was brought back for the return match against the Portuguese side. We pulled back two goals and I scored the third, a header, and then I was out of the team again.

It made no difference. I was out in the cold. The winter passed without my playing and at Easter, with John Richards injured, I saw that I was included as substitute in the first team squad at White Hart Lane. I played for the last twenty minutes and did reasonably well.

I was in the side for the next match, over the Easter period against Manchester City, which we won. The following Monday McGarry sent for me. I had played only a handful of games all season. 'How do you want to finish your playing career, in the first team or reserves?' he asked. It was not an invitation, for he went on. 'I'm not going to play you any more in the first team.' My last game had been against Manchester City at Molineux. I had finished. Just like that. I had played my last game for Wolves and at the time I had not known it. It had been decided for me and I was told two days after the event.

Good grief! Was this how it had to end? Was this the way to treat a seasoned professional who had done his best for his club? I had set a record as the first Irishman to score 200 goals in the English League, passing Peter Doherty's total of 199. And I had broken the European record held by Peter Broadbent in his heyday with Wolves. Denis Law and Dennis Viollet were the only two other players to score nine goals in European competition in one season, a new record of ten goals was later set up by Stan Bowles playing for Queen's Park Rangers.

I could justly claim that I had paid my way at Wolves and my partnership with John Richards had been acclaimed in the first division. None of these contributions and achievements was mentioned. I was just another has-been, no longer wanted for the first team squad and it was up to me what I did,

108

quit or play in the reserves. Was this how it was to end? Were my years and my service at Wolves to count for nothing in the end?

It was a sad way to go, because I had anticipated taking my leave before the Molineux crowd in the last game of the season, a crowd with whom I had enjoyed a happy, wonderful, relationship. It seemed I was to be denied this pleasure. And I would have been, had pressure not been exerted in influential quarters.

The day before the final home match of the season I received a phone call from Alan Williams, the *Daily Express* sports reporter. 'Congratulations,' he said. 'What for?' 'You're in the squad tomorrow to play Leeds.'

I was in the first team squad through the intervention of what I might call 'public pressure'. Questions had been asked, particularly in the local press. An undercurrent of feeling had built up and McGarry was obliged to include me in the squad. But I had to sit on the substitute's bench until twelve minutes from time, when I was brought on. There was no time for me to get into my stride, no time to get involved in the game and make a fitting departure. It was nothing more than a token farewell performance, with a strict time limit. When he told me to get stripped and go on, I should have told him to get lost. In the event I allowed him to humiliate me because I did not want to offend the biggest crowd of the season who had come to pay their last respects.

Afterwards, in the boardroom, Harry Marshall the present Chairman and other directors shook hands and thanked me. There was no sign of Bill McGarry. He kept out of the way and I left the ground without a word from him. More than 35,000 people attended the match. There were emotional scenes and I waved farewell to supporters, blowing kisses to them, I could scarcely hold back the tears. When a player takes his leave, after years of service, the one person he expects to be there to say goodbye and wish him well in the future, is his manager.

My 'crime', it seems, was being popular with the crowd. After the final whistle I did not see much of Bill McGarry until a sportsmen's committee, with which I was involved, held a private dinner party in December at a local hotel in my honour.

109

Before the coffee was served, he left. Not a word that he was taking his leave.

Three months after my retirement Wolves were playing at home to Queen's Park Rangers and wanting to speak to QPR's manager, Dave Sexton, I went to the ground, only to be told by the Wolves secretary, Phil Shaw, that I could not enter the reception area. 'What's all this about?' I asked. He told me the manager wanted to see me. 'What about?' He said he would leave it to Mr McGarry to tell me. When I persisted he explained that Mr McGarry had given instruction that if I came to the ground I was not to be permitted to go into the reception area.

Although I was offered a complimentary ticket for any game, I have never taken advantage of the offer. There is no point in my accepting favours when there is not sufficient goodwill behind them. Being sensitive to atmosphere, I did not need a geiger counter to detect an undercurrent of hostility towards me – or, if not hostility, a certain amount of resentment stemming from the McGarry era.

The following 9 March 1976, I was asked by the BBC to provide comments for a broadcast of an FA Cup replay at Molineux, against Manchester United. I was to come in now and again to sum up play and make my own observations, from a seat in the directors' box. The BBC asked for three tickets. Normally, they asked for two. When they were asked who the third ticket was for and they gave my name, the barrier went up. They were told I could not be admitted to the directors' box, but no reason was given. To do the broadcast comments I had to sit with the spectators in the stand and leave the game to hurry to the operations room below the Waterloo Road stand to get to the microphone.

From there it was not possible to see any of the game and I had to backtrack, commenting on what I had seen until leaving my seat.

Was I being singled out for snubbing? I sensed Bill McGarry's hand on the 'no entry' signs, but it is a fact that once players have finished playing they are not always treated by their former clubs with the friendliness and respect they deserve. Quite often they are treated as embarrassing has-beens, to be shrugged off. When they are no longer of use to

110

the club, they are rarely made to feel welcomed. I have seen plenty of 'old and faithful servants' paying at the turnstiles and standing on the terraces at the clubs where they were once idols and to which they devoted their careers.

I am sure the atmosphere at Molineux would have been more receptive if Bill McGarry had gone to Coventry, as seemed likely in the close season of 1972. I well remember the reaction of most of the players when he took Mike Bailey aside after the second leg of a UEFA Cup final at Spurs and told him he was going to Coventry. When Bailey passed the message to the players there was an audible sigh of relief, followed by singing and chanting on the team coach.

For some reason the deal fell through and McGarry stayed until the lamentable fall into the second division, which would never have happened if he had bought the right players at the right time and made the best use of the players on his books. I know I could have played a part in avoiding relegation, just as I had in winning promotion. In my last two seasons I could have helped myself by 'cooling it' in training and not trying to train like a sixteen-year-old. Had I been able to anticipate the decline and demotion to the second division I would have had the operation on my back to get fully fit for the struggle and I would have stayed on.

It would have been better in the circumstances if I had reserved some of my energy for match days, but my pride insisted on competing with younger players in training and doing far more than was necessary. And yet, it would probably not have made any difference, given Bill McGarry's determination to replace me.

This was how it was at Wolves. There is an old Bing Crosby–Bob Hope joke, one saying there is nothing they would not do for one another and adding: 'We've spent all our lives doing nothing for one another.' I could go one better. There was nothing I would not do for Bill McGarry on and off the pitch, for the benefit of Wolves. But it seemed there was nothing he would do for me. Not once in all the years of his management at Wolves could he bring himself to call me by christian name. It was always 'Big man' or 'Dougan'.

During Ronnie Allen's time I could have gone to Coventry, whose manager, Noel Cantwell, was willing to buy me. After the news had broken in a Sunday newspaper, Wolves chairman John Ireland told me there was no way I would be leaving Molineux. I said to him: 'I've been waiting all my career for a chairman to tell me that,' and I repeated my hope and determination to stay with Wolves to the end of my playing career. The upshot was that I signed a six-year contract, which I think stuck in the gullet of McGarry when he took over. In my seven years under the McGarry regime, I averaged over fifteen goals a season – and that includes the time I was under suspension and recovering from injuries. A manager would give his eyeteeth for a player these days who could guarantee such a scoring rate. But I never had a word of thanks from the Boss, not one word of appreciation in all that time. Nor did I get a penny in wages when I was suspended by the Football Association disciplinary body, even though I attended training sessions every day. Of course, the system meant suspension without pay. Later the PFA secretary, Cliff Lloyd, battled and succeeded in changing the procedure, so that players under suspension continued to be paid, but did not receive bonuses. Even so, everyone in the game knew there were ways and means of 'getting round' the system. There were no favours for me from McGarry. Sometimes, after brooding on the distant relationship between us and the knowledge that whatever I did, I could never 'get on the right side' of him, I would bang my fists on the wall at home and kick out at the furniture in frustration and despair because I could not get back at him.

Eight

If there had been any poetic justice, Birmingham City and not Wolves would have been relegated on 4 May 1976. Birmingham were perennial first division strugglers, forever putting up a last ditch fight to avoid the drop. It should have been their turn.

The Football League arranged matters with scrupulous fairness, with Birmingham away at Sheffield United and Wolves at home to Liverpool on the same fateful night. Wolves had to win and Birmingham lose for the Wanderers to stay up. Even if the Wolves had overcome Liverpool, instead of being overrun in the last quarter, it would have made no difference as Birmingham drew at Sheffield.

Many years before Molineux crowds uprooted the goalposts in their anger when the club was relegated. This time there was no sorrow, just acceptance of the inevitable. I felt that few people really cared. My sadness turned to incredulity and anger not long afterwards when the club handed Bill McGarry almost £32,000 to end his contract.

Exactly what had been achieved in his eight years at Molineux? We had won the League Cup and the Texaco Cup. The odd time we had seriously challenged for the championship. And yet, although I finished my career without a first division championship medal or an FA Cup Winners' trophy, I was pleased to have been with Wolves. Of all my clubs it was the one with which I most closely identified myself.

Life is made up of chances, fate and circumstances. In 1961, when I was with Blackburn Rovers, the Belgian Club Anderlecht wanted to sign me for £20,000 and I was willing to go. Before a contract was signed they began arguing about the fee. They suggested that if they could get me for less, I would be given a little more. This was in the days of the maximum wage.

113

Looking back, I was pleased it did not work out, because for me the English League is the only competitive league in the world that really matters.

If I had gone to Anderlecht, I would not have met my wife in Birmingham ... If I hadn't met her at a critical time in my career, when I was thoroughly depressed at Aston Villa, I would have fallen out of the game. She helped me to take a grip on myself and use the third division (Peterborough) as a springboard back into the first division and the Northern Ireland Squad.

I needed that grip at Wolves when I would otherwise have been demoralised by Bill McGarry's attitude towards me. On numerous occasions he refused permission for me to be interviewed by sports writers and broadcasters, telling them that they could have anyone but me. I know, because they came to me first and I had to tell them to get his permission but not to mention that they had already spoken to me.

At a lesser club I would have walked out. I stayed because Wolverhampton Wanderers meant everything to me and it is still the club I admire above all others. It has not yet found the successful route to newfound glories; it cannot yet compete with the memories of the fifties. But it retains an aura and as I said in my first book *Attack!*; it could well be that the best days are yet to come.

A lot of supporters, with years of experience, usually know what is wrong and what is right with a club. They don't have to eavesdrop at board meetings or pick up the dressing-room gossip. They sense it. Managers and directors could learn a lot by mingling, anonymously, on the terraces. But would they know how to put into practice what they learn there, among the fans? More to the point, would they have the nerve to do it, if this meant abandoning the cherished illusions and prejudices?

In my career I have met a few imaginative managers, open-minded and generous in spirit. But they are far outnumbered by those whose basic insecurity has clouded their vision and caused them to forget what it is like to be a player. I don't want to forget what it's like, in whatever I do in the future, which is one of the reasons why management in its present state has not appealed to me.

114

A great manager – and there haven't been too many this century – has confidence in himself without the arrogance of conceit and his confidence is transmitted to his players, who will play their hearts out for him. A mediocre manager tries to will the success he does not know how to achieve through merit and he blames his players when he fails. His players know that he will abuse them if they lose the match and that he'll bellow at them like a belligerent sergeant-major at the training sessions or ignore them as they pass in the corridor between his office and the dressing room. It's childish for a man, possibly in his forties, to walk past a player without speaking. Players will never play their hearts out for such a man. Their hearts will be heavy, as if dragging leaden weights around the pitch.

I have had my share of mediocre, uninspiring, and temperamental managers in my time. My early reputation as a trouble-maker came partly from my need to raise myself above the demoralising influences they exerted. If I hadn't done this I am convinced I would have gone under with them, and been lost to the game.

We hear managers saying that players need discipline. What they don't say is that players, like anyone in any other profession, need self-discipline. What they are saying is that in their opinion players are unintelligent children or juveniles who cannot be trusted to discipline themselves and like to be ordered about. I have never liked being told what to do, whether I was eighteen or thirty-six. I prefer to be asked, which is a trait few managers in my experience have been able to understand. They – and still I'm generalising – cling to the old traditions, which insisted on treating players as lackeys and managers as overlords. Social barriers that have broken down in society are often slow to fall in football clubs.

In what other profession would someone at managerial level dare to impose a heavy fine on an employee who had been seen in a night club or a pub a few nights before a professional engagement?

This has happened time and again in football, where a player has gone out to relax at a bar or a nightspot. If a player is abusing his physique it will show in his performance and he won't be sharp enough to keep his place. But it does not follow that his physique will in any way be ruined by socialising a

115

couple of nights before a match. Some may play better. It depends entirely on their constitution. I know an ex-international player who used to share a dozen bottles of beer with a team mate on the night before any away game. Both players went on to play for almost twenty years. Incidentally, they both went on to become managers, one in the first division, the other in the second.

I mention this as one example of the petty tyrannies that survive. Disciplinary rules vary from club to club. There are no overall standard procedures. Most of these rules are determined by the whims of individual managers. One will come down heavily on players who turn up on match days without wearing ties. Another will crack down with fines on players who are a few minutes late for training. I remember two players being sent home to put on a tie and jacket. They could have got their own back by returning in just those two items and nothing more – I wish they had – but obediently they did just as they were told, knowing that refusal would have meant a fine or some other form of disciplinary action. I also saw the same manager send a couple of players home to shave. It's strange, but you never hear of mass rebellion, anarchy or reaction at clubs against such pettiness. It shows how much discipline there is among players. What I admired about Gordon Clark was that he never asked any of his Peterborough players to do what he wasn't prepared to do himself, and he treated us as men.

There may be clubs where managers and players are as one, on the same wavelength, pooling their ideas for the common good. I'm afraid there aren't many. The hierarchical system is such that players even now, in spite of the abolition of the maximum wage, remain in relative serfdom, told to get on with the game and leave the rest to the boss. It's as if managements fear an outbreak of players' power or a 'players' co-operative'. Players should be treated as equals and given their say.

This explains why, so often in my career, I was branded as an upstart when all I was trying to do was impart my judgment and express my views.

Silent subservience has always been unnatural to me, I've observed it at first hand among fellow players who have been embarrassed when I've spoken up and edged further away on the dressing-room benches to avoid being associated with my so-called radical opinions.

Old systems die hard. Players emerged as lesser breeds within a structured administration supervised by the 'gentlemen amateurs' and to some extent this atmosphere lingers. I have known players in awe of their managers, like schoolboys fearful of disciplinarian headmasters. And I've experienced managers who made it a mission of life to bring me to heel, resenting me simply for being myself, scarcely able to contain their rage when I've been involved in publicity, no matter how beneficial that publicity was to the club. Possibly they took the view that they and not the players were to initiate any publicity and that if a player was involved in 'limelight' publicity it was engineered for his own benefit. It's a short-sighted view. Many players are fearful of anything appearing in the press about them without managerial blessing, thus depriving clubs of useful public relations.

My only regret about playing for Wolves is that I was not able to play for them in the days of those two scintillating wingers – Hancocks and Mullen. Given the choice, I would have chosen their period, rather than mine, even though it was not until after they had finished that players began to get their just reward with the ending of the maximum wage.

In football you are only as good as your last game. If you have a succession of good games and a successful season, winning cups (domestic or European) and the league, then you are achieving all that can be achieved. You're at the top of your profession and of your own capabilities. Wolves would have suited me in those days because of the wing service I would have enjoyed from Hancocks and Mullen. I would have revelled in their crosses and in the success of the side in the league, Cup competitions and in non-competitive European matches. They still talk in Wolverhampton, and elsewhere, of those glorious achievements at Molineux twenty-five years ago. How I wish I could have shared in them as part of that winning side, which thrilled thousands and made the name of Wolves famous throughout the world. But even as a 'late comer', I was pleased to join Wolves.

There were scoffs and knowing winks when I said, in the press, that I wished to end my playing career at Molineux.

117

Sceptics predicted that I would be on my way again within two years. That was more than ten years ago. I honoured my pledge. I was lucky in finding the club where I could express myself despite the internal situation. The irony is that I did so after completing the span which is the average playing life of a footballer. I was given a re-birth in football at a stage when, by the law of average, I should have been hanging up my boots. Wolves and not McGarry re-charged my batteries and gave me the stimulus I needed to more than double the average playing life.

In many ways my years at Molineux have been the most exciting, fruitful and rewarding of my career, coinciding with my chairmanship of the PFA and the publication of a novel – *The Footballer* – in which I tried to personify and summarise the pressures at work within the game and the increasing demands put on the stars before they have gained maturity. People have asked if I had Wolves in mind when describing Branton United in the novel and whether the hero, Danny Stone, is a self-portrait.

I had in mind various clubs and various players, who have merged in my mind as a kind of sum-total. Being with a side such as Wolves gives one a focus for the game in general. It is old-established and became internationally renowned in the fifties, when the might of Europe was humbled at Molineux. My most creative years have been spent with Wolves, not without traumas and disappointments – but what is football or life without them anyway?

What I most regret about Wolves during my period there is that we did not have two orthodox wingers.

Although I had a productive scoring record, I could have done much more with a two-wing service. There were times, especially in away games, when I was left upfield by myself in the hope of collecting the ball in a breakaway and going through by myself.

As I said earlier, the breakdown in standard wing play on both flanks began about fifteen years ago. Until then a winger's customary role was to wait in position on his wing, and when he received a pass, to streak down the wing, centre the ball or cut in with it for a shot. That's the way so many superb Wolves goals came in the fifties. In recent years Wolves have operated

118

with one orthodox winger, David Wagstaffe, who at his peak has justified comparison with the great raiding wingmen and has not had the national recognition he deserves. If he had been recognised by Alf Ramsey and given an opportunity to show what he could do in the England side, he would have had greater belief in himself. I wish Alf had had the courage to do this. After all, for example, Jack Charlton spent a number of years in comparative obscurity before getting his chance, because of the successful Leeds team, in the England side. I considered it a cardinal sin that Waggy never played for his country and was only recognised in an English League side. He and a lot more are victims of a system which virtually dispensed with wingers at the time the game was being enamoured by such clichés as 'work-rate' and 'getting men behind the ball'.

It is, when you think about it, common sense to say that managers ought to find styles of play that suit their players. But the game is not always noted for common sense. It is too often noted for rigid thinking and slavish addiction to techniques that have somehow become fashionable.

The game changes because it evolves. It also changes because managers and coaches try to graft on to it artificial styles that the game, as a corporate body, later rejects. I don't want to delve back too far and make irrelevant comparisons between the game today and the game as it was played half a century ago. That would be like comparing Muhammad Ali with Jack Johnson. But there have been more changes on the pitch since 1953 than in any other period since 1863 when the rules were drawn up.

A major turning point came when the Hungarians beat England at Wembley, in 1953 6–3, a result considered to be just one of those freaks, until a little later that season when the Hungarians in Budapest rubbed the lesson home, 7–1.

The Hungarians taught English football that by a player changing his shirt number the opposition can be thrown into disarray. We were used to conventional formations in which the centre-half picked up the rival centre forward, the left-back marked the right winger and so on. The Hungarians' no. 9 played a deep lying role taking the centre-half, Billy Wright, by surprise. The result – havoc in the England side. I remember vividly how the tactics of Freddie Cox at Portsmouth confused the opposition by changing numbers on players' backs, but unfortunately in his case, it also confused his own players.

Gradually, over the years, as the game quickened, trainers and coaches fell under the spell of new, scientific jargon – cutting space, quick tackling and close marking became the foremost methods of stopping attacks.

Leeds, under Don Revie, demonstrated these methods to perfection, wearing down the opposition and putting emphasis on defence. They were inclined to be too mechanical to rouse the crowds and have not managed to build up the sort of support enjoyed by Liverpool and Manchester United, which are more positive in attack and more adventurous.

People came from long distances to pay homage to the best in British football under the lights of Molineux. It's a generation since the heyday of Billy Wright, captain of Wolves and England, but the heroes of those days are still revered and remain fresh in the minds of those who saw them humble the greatest sides in Europe. I would have liked a similar sort of perpetuation. It is almost twenty years since I asked for a transfer on the eve of a Cup Final and also shaved my head, but this is what a lot of people remember me by, not as the longest serving playing chairman of the PFA since the war, not as a centre forward who played at Wembley against Wolves in the 1960 FA Cup Final and then at Wembley for Wolves in the 1974 League Cup Final. I have made the most of my time and my place in the game, but romantically I day-dream of what memories I might have had and how I would be remembered if I had been fortunate enough to be with Wolves in the fifties, playing against Honved, Spartak and the rest (by the way, whatever became of the Hungarians?).

Wolves were a kind of last bastion, not only holding the fort against overwhelming attacks from Eastern Europe but repulsing the enemy in spectacular style. By the introduction of floodlights, in the early fifties, Wolves attracted foreign opposition for evening games and packed the ground to capacity. Fast raiding wingers and effective use of the long ball demoralised oppositions. Other English teams, of course, tried to emulate, Wolves. Others were more circumspect and cut their coats according to their cloth. Manchester United, Wolves'

120

closest rivals in the fifties, did not have the same kind of players to use the same system and they stuck to short and long balls. Spurs, in their cultured football, were a mixture of Wolves and United. Liverpool, under Bill Shankly and then Bob Paisley, have been pre-eminent, proving that success depends on having the same manager for a long period and establishing consistency – as with Bill Nicholson at Spurs, Don Revie at Leeds, Matt Busby of Manchester United.

Turning back to Sir Alf, after he had won the first division championship for Ipswich, with virtually unknown players, some of them cast-offs, Alf was given the England job. He devised a plan to win the World Cup – a plan that had no place for the mercurial, goal-poaching skill of Jimmy Greaves.

No sooner had Alf's tactic worked, than League clubs were rushing to identify themselves with the method. A bandwagon was set in motion and all manner of managers were trying to leap on it. If Alf could do it at international level, they could do it at club level. His plan had been put into operation and it had worked. There could be no argument with that. England had a trophy to prove the case – and Alf had done it without wingers.

Most league managers are conformists. If Alf had won with wingers I am completely convinced they would have encouraged wing play.

It just didn't occur to them that to be successful in their own spheres as Alf Ramsey was in his, they needed exactly the same kind of players. Nor did it occur to them that Alf's rigid tactics would eventually bring about his downfall and that he would be criticised for unimaginative strategy in which his players were not able to express themselves.

Success cannot be repeated here, there and everywhere by adopting the means of that success. For instance take Don Howe. At Arsenal, when the gunners won the double, he was regarded as the chief architect of the feat and his reputation as the best coach in the country (Malcolm Allison would have told you otherwise) led to his appointment as manager of West Bromwich. The thinking at The Hawthorns was that he could achieve there what he had achieved at Highbury. How could the country's foremost coach, now a manager, possibly fail?

He, above all men in the game, knew not only what had to be done but how to do it. Unfortunately, for Don Howe, he could not take all the Arsenal players with him and West Bromwich were relegated to the second division. A manager or coach is no better than the players under him. Does the coach make the team or the team the coach? Perhaps both, through inter-reaction.

The trouble with many managers is they don't try to understand their own players and they are not willing to learn from them.

I've never been any manager's blue-eyed boy and only two managers, Gordon Clark and Eddie Lever, have shown me that they really liked me, or I felt they liked me. Most have regarded me from various points of view ranging from suspicion to hostility, when all I've wanted was to be helpful and be helped!

It is difficult for a player to make a suggestion, no matter how constructive, without arousing suspicion or hostility. There is a widespread feeling that players cannot or should not be trusted when talking of matters that affect the teams. At Molineux I told successive managers that Gordon Banks would be a sound investment, that Tommy Hutchinson would be a good acquisition for the club when he was at Blackpool, that Ray Graydon would be more than an asset if he could be bought from Aston Villa. Unfortunately, my suggestions fell on deaf ears. After a while I decided that there was no point in trying to make useful suggestions.

My reasoning is, as a striker, in pleading the cause of right and left wingers was simple. If you are getting a good service from one wing, why not double the prospects with equal service from the other wing? The need for strike forces from the wings has become more imperative, not less, since the days of tight defensive formations began with Leeds under Don Revie and England under Alf Ramsey. It should be obvious that if attacks are being stifled by quick tackling and close marking, the best manœuvre and counter-move is to operate down the wings and in those parts of the pitch that cannot be 'policed'. Defences cannot afford to deploy men in the corner areas. It is here that attacks can find room and where attacks can be propelled. Oppositions cannot cut out both sides of the pitch.

There was I, a tall striker able to reach with my head high balls floating over defences, being left in the middle without the service my physique and style demanded. With Waggy out of the team on occasions through injury, I did not get proper service. I have played many games without a single cross in ninety minutes and that's a frustrating experience for a player who likes nothing better than to head home a well-placed centre.

There is discrimination against forward play by some clubs, who put their faith in defence, their hope in breakaway attack and haven't enough charity for spectators who have to put up with the effects. What might appear, on paper, to be an exciting pulsating match can be reduced by negative thinking to stupefying tedium. One example of this was the FA Cup tie second replay – which I went to see – between Leicester City and Arsenal in the 1974–5 season at Filbert Street. But overall the game to me is more exciting than it's ever been in the past. It has more skill, players are sharper and more athletic.

In that Leicester City–Arsenal match both sides played the tight marking, quick tackling tactic and played it well; so well that no creative football could develop. It was as if the players had lost their way in no-man's land, without a compass. The trouble is that in the circumstances the tactics made sense. Neither side could allow the other to seize a creative advantage. It was a case of destroying every move before it could lead somewhere. No doubt the players had to be nimble in thought and deed but the effect was boring for spectators. How, then, can you put up a case against what was logical, as a better plan? The only answer is that clubs must consider what the game is all about. It is a spectacle which cannot exist without spectators. Games are not played in isolation. They are played for the benefit of the public, who must be entertained. There are games when one questions if they are negative, defensive, boring, aggressive, brilliant or exciting and everyone has a different point of view. This is what makes it the greatest game in the world, or as Paddy Crerand says, 'the only game'.

What can be done to make the game more entertaining? I have already set out my views about the negative offside rule, the most niggling and destructive rule in the book, encouraging defences to move up in a solid line to the half way circle. Its abolition would bring greater fluency and attack into the game.

Few people realise that a player is offside if he is in exact line with the rival defender who has put him offside. The common belief is that he can only be offside if he is behind a defender when the ball is played to him. Many linesmen raise their flags for offside according to where a player is when he receives the ball, not where he was when the ball was played. This enrages supporters as much as players.

As I have already said, 'open-plan' football has made the offside rule superfluous. Possibly there was a case for it in the days of the old formations, when teams stuck to two full-backs, three half-backs and five forwards. Now, with full-backs overlapping and attackers falling back to defend, I insist that offside is meaningless.

The game would benefit enormously from its abolition. Play would be opened out, with greater room for manœuvre. Players would be able to use the whole pitch, which is what the pitch is for, instead of bunching in mid-field.

I repeat my plea for another change in the introduction of direct shots and the defensive line-up be scrapped outside the penalty box. Time and again a player is going through only to be hauled down or tripped yards, even inches, outside the penalty area. And what happens? The referee gives a free kick, the opposition packs the goal area and advantage is lost; unless there is a super-shot player who can 'bend' the ball for a banana shot over the defence and out of the goalkeeper's reach.

The so-called 'professional' foul just outside the penalty area persists because the offenders know that all they risk is a booking. Generally, they get away with a finger wagging and feel satisfied that they have prevented the other side from scoring. If such fouls were penalised by direct shots at goal, with only the goalkeeper to beat, the professional foul would no longer favour the side which commits it.

I would also like to see all League clubs forming players' committees, consisting of a club's chairman or a director, manager and three players (the captain, a senior and a junior player). Committees could discuss players behaviour on and off the pitch, team performances and whatever else concerns the club. (In this respect, we could learn a lesson from cricket, where the team captain is very much involved in selection and all the real important issues affecting his sport.)

So far I know only a few clubs that have this kind of committee. A lot of managers are not easily swayed in favour of this idea, they see it as a threat to their overall authority. They would probably have responded enthusiastically when they were players, but when they become managers they undergo a Jekyll and Hyde transformation. If they thought about it more carefully, they would see such committees as a means of releasing their own tensions and channelling their ideas. They would no longer feel isolated – and it is the isolation of managers, caught in a limbo between players (their subordinates) and boards of directors (their overlords), that affects their nervous systems.

They are inclined to be laws unto themselves, self-styled oracles who will deliver judgments but rarely listen to counter-arguments. It is as if by nature of the job a manager is expected to be a repository of soccer wisdom and master supreme, to be kicked out when he fails to make good his promise. Fewer managers would lose their jobs if they worked in co-operation with their players and listened to constructive suggestions by those who are directly involved in putting managerial policy into practice.

I begin to lose respect for managers and coaches when they go off their heads and say they don't rate the likes of Alan Hudson, Peter Osgood, Martin Chivers, Stanley Bowles, Tony Currie and Malcolm MacDonald to name but a few. I have heard some of the most talented players in the game being 'put down' behind their backs by various managers, who say (or pretend) they wouldn't want them in their teams and wouldn't even take them on free transfers. That's not judgment, it is prejudice. Yet these are the men at the helm of the profession, the men who decide which way the game goes, the men who tell the players what to do and how to do it. It was Talleyrand, said Lloyd George, who said 'that war was too serious to be left to military men'. Sometimes I think football is too serious to be left to managers.

125

Nine

Responsibility is something you have to learn. I learned it the hard way. They say that with age cometh wisdom. It doesn't follow, though it's certainly true that a thirty-year-old doesn't behave like a twenty-year-old. There trouble was that by the time I had reached thirty many people inside the game expected me to behave as I had when I was twenty. There is an 'ageless' quality about football. From the stands and terraces footballers have an indeterminate appearance, where age is concerned. Their movements, rather than their features, characterise them and they are expected to move with the same fluency and rhythm whatever their age. Most players, on the pitch, look about twenty-four to twenty-eight. Even if they are twenty or thirty-five.

But inwardly I knew I was changing and beginning to appreciate the process of maturity. The process began when I was invited to join the PFA committee. This confirmed that if the players' union could take me seriously enough to have me on the committee, I could take myself seriously when there was still a popular view that I was too much of a showman to demonstrate any responsibility where it mattered most.

Another player who joined the committee at the same time as me was Terry Neill. Two years later the chairman, Noel Cantwell, vacated office in 1967 to take over as manager of Coventry City. It crossed my mind that I could be in the running to succeed him. Maurice Setters was the more senior committee man, but his track record was against him and he knew it. Because of his disciplinary record on the pitch he decided to rule himself out. In my view he would have been an excellent chairman. He had enthusiasm and dedication. He wanted to do all he could to improve the welfare and conditions of players. What more is required in a chairman of the PFA? I felt it should not have mattered how many bookings he had had as a player, but it did.

No doubt he sensed that the committee would give paramount importance to the 'image' of its chairman and for this reason would not elect him. He saved the committee the embarrassment of having to consider him and it was between me and Terry Neill.

At an hotel in Manchester in November prior to the AGM of the PFA we were asked to leave the room while the committee deliberated. We waited in the corridor, making hard work of conversation. When we were called back the expression on Noel Cantwell's face told me I had not been elected. Terry Neill was chosen because he represented what was required, a nice, pleasant image. My behaviour on the pitch between 1957 and 1967 had been taken into account and had clearly gone against me. One sending off at Nottingham when I was with Aston Villa and a number of cautions.

My behaviour on the pitch in this period did not relate to my sense of responsibility off it. I was still considered somewhat headstrong when compared with Terry Neill.

The next two years and nine months were exasperating for me. Working with him, not under him, I could have beaten my head against the nearest goalposts when negotiations and discussions with the Football League and the Football Association put the PFA in the position of forelock touching. Terry, who had never been in trouble with referees and radiated a clean-cut aura, seemed anxious to build on his 'nice guy' reputation. Not wanting to offend anyone, he became in my opinion, too deferential for the hurly burly of negotiation. There were important polices the PFA wanted implementing and we were dealing with football authorities steeped in tradition and a somewhat condescending attitude towards players.

Tough, respectful talking was required; hard negotiating was essential. Quite often I found myself, with Cliff Lloyd, doing most of the talking, but I did not have the authority of the chair. It was like being in the Cabinet, feeling able to do the Prime Minister's job and yet enfeebled through lack of authority. It wasn't a matter of power-mongering, only of wishing desperately for the opportunity to lead the party I represented for the good of members. As a committee member, I could not appear too forceful; nor did I want to appear radical.

For as long as I can remember, I have always been my own

127

man. It was in my background. East Belfast was a hard conditioner. Either you succumbed to the environment or you tried to rise above it. You could give in to the sectarian bigotry, as a way of life, and spend the rest of your days living out the fantasies and prejudices; or you could use your imagination and get away, all the time learning from early experiences and recognising the importance of developing mind and body. If you did not want to be like so many others, narrow in vision, you had to be yourself. I had an advantage with height, which enabled me to get above most rival players and reach the high balls. I felt that a part of the pitch, six feet two inches or more, belonged to me; a world apart and mine to control.

Chairmanship of the PFA, I knew, would give me an extra dimension in which to express myself on behalf of the association which had become my way of life. That is why I was so exasperated at times in negotiations and wanted to put words into Terry Neill's mouth.

Just over two years later exasperation turned to relief and elation in 1970 when Terry resigned from the Committee to become player-manager of Hull City. The committee agreed unanimously that I should be the next chairman. Although Bobby Charlton, who had the cleanest possible record – even cleaner than Terry Neill's – was on the committee, my name was the only one proposed, in spite of my having been sent off twice within three weeks only nine months previously. Those summary dismissals, at Sheffield Wednesday's ground and at Molineux against Everton, gave me the distinction of being the only first division player since the 1920s to be sent off twice in three weeks. It was reassuring, therefore, to know that the PFA committee considered me the man for the job. The appointment prompted me to evaluate my pitch behaviour. Most of my bookings in the past had just been for talking back to referees. Now that I was chairman of the players' union I knew that I could not let my emotional reaction to anything that happened in a game, lead me into conflict with the refs. I had to do all I could to set a good example. At the same time one has to admit that bookings can be professional hazards, dogging a player's footsteps. Since being elected chairman – and becoming the longest-serving chairman of the PFA since the war – I have had only two bookings in six years.

128

Whatever I gained in responsibility as chairman, I owe much to the PFA's secretary Cliff Lloyd, and its solicitor George Davies, whose sincerity, integrity and sense of values gave me the inspiration and stimulus I needed. Their qualities rubbed off a little, enabling me to mature in office. But I soon felt the ambiguity of my new position. The chairmanship of an association carries with it authority as well as responsibility. By virtue of office, I was on equal terms with the chairmen of other football bodies. But as a player I was still subservient to those bodies.

I have had to act with considerable restraint and go about my duties in a way that could not upset my own club or the League. All the time I have been aware that should I, as chairman, speak out of turn or say something the authorities considered outlandish, the hierarchy could say: 'What's that bloody Dougan talking about? Tell him to belt up.'

I have never sought power for its own sake and have tried, when presiding over meetings at which players' working conditions have been discussed, to emphasise the importance of negotiations with the football authorities. Nothing has angered me more than to see the phrase 'players demand' in sports headlines. The PFA has made a great deal of progress over the past twenty years, but has never once demanded anything. Ours is probably the only large industry in Britain which has never resorted to strike action or other forms of industrial action. The word 'demand' is not in our lexicon. We propose and discussions are followed by negotiations, and persuasion. In a game run at the top, by dilettantes who do not get their living from it, industrial action by the professionals who rely on it for their living, would achieve nothing. It would only jeopardise the livelihoods of the bread-and-butter players, particularly those in the lower divisions – and it is they whom the PFA gives priority (if there should be priority given).

If we are to make even more rapid progress, the PFA's constitution should be changed to enable committee members to be given a day off from their clubs every week to attend to PFA business and get to grips with all the issues involved. Or maybe even considering adopting the Dutch system in which ex-players retain positions of importance. Too much depends on grace and favour by individual clubs, with no sure guarantee

129

of a committee member or PFA delegate being released to conduct his union's business, especially at annual general meetings. For the record I know of a number of cases where managers deliberately wouldn't let the PFA delegate have the time off to attend the AGM.

Nor has the PFA been on absolutely equal terms with the League and FA when it comes to discussing important issues affecting its members. Too much is decided by the other bodies without the PFA being asked to contribute its views, although the position is beginning to improve, as the association raises its prestige and status, through its achievements.

In recent years the PFA has been able to claim considerable progress for all its members such as the percentage a player gets from his transfer fee and the improvements in the disciplinary machinery. The case of an unknown player called John Cook, who went to play in Southern Ireland, highlighted a maddening anomaly. When he returned to England the FA refused to register him. The PFA supported the player in a test case and established the right of a player to return and play in his own country when he has fulfilled the conditions of his contract in another country.

The PFA can take pride in getting all the football authorities around the same negotiating table. It is only a few years since the first tri-partite meeting in the game's history – Football League, FA and PFA. Such meetings are infrequent, but they have been established.

Of the two big issues at the time of writing, one has been settled – a qualified freedom of contract. The other is a pension scheme for all members of the PFA. It is only a matter of time before the last hurdle is surmounted. Various managers and clubs opposed freedom of contract because they believed it would destroy the game. They fought a rear guard action against irresistible progress. The old system was a relic of serfdom, with players being bought and sold at the market. The transfer system is humiliating and a financial burden on the league. In effect, it is a restraint of movement still and has no legal or moral justification. Given freedom of contract, players will enjoy what is taken for granted in other professions. It ought to have been a basic right long ago, but football is an institution which is slow to throw off vestiges of the master–

servant relationship that existed when the League was formed in the last century.

We still speak of a long-serving player being 'a good and faithful servant' of his club, instead of an employee or member.

The managerial theory is that with freedom of contract players would be scurrying from club to club and the best clubs would get all the best players. They said this before the maximum wage was abolished. It didn't happen then and would not happen under freedom of contract, because the 'best' club for one particular player could be the 'worst' club for another. Players like to be settled and they will prefer to stay with the club which looks after their interests and can assure them of first team places. Movements would be no greater than they are now, under the transfer system. Managers have freedom to move, when their contracts expire. In fact, they don't always wait for their contracts to end. I don't see why players should not have similar rights.

I suspect the die-hard managers, fearful of losing their overall authority, want to keep players in bondage.

The image of a footballer as a thick-headed yokel, who needs constant discipline and cannot be trusted to manage his own affairs, is a distant throw-back. The real image belongs to the PFA awards night, which I helped, with Eric Woodward of Aston Villa and Cliff Lloyd, to inaugurate in March 1974. The television cameras, roaming casually through groups of dinner jacketed players, waiting to go into dinner, have presented nationwide a more articulate, self-assured image. It could never have entered the imaginations of players in the old days to visualise members of the Royal Family or the Prime Minister as guest of honour, presenting awards, at a dinner organised by the players organisation. Anyone who doubts the social progress of the modern footballer has only to switch on the Player of the Year award on ITV, without doubt the best night on the sporting calendar.

There was a lot of controversy about the idea. A few cynical sports writers said it would be nothing more than self back-slapping, showing how indulgent players were becoming towards one another. They seemed to forget their own awards to fellow members of the newspaper profession – News Reporter

131

of the Year, Columnist of the Year, Feature Writer of the Year ... At least ours is more democratic. In the newspaper world awards are decided by a small committee and I daresay a great deal of lobbying is done behind the scenes.

Footballers choose their recipients not by committee but through votes – and every player in the league has a vote. Further, our awards night is attended by well over 500 past and present footballers. At the Footballer of the Year dinners I have attended, organised by sports writers and held before the FA Cup Final, I have never seen more than a handful of players among the guests – and I'm still looking for a number of third and fourth division players. And then they had the gall to question the motives of the players' own Player of the Year! There is room for both awards, from outside and from inside the game. We might end up with footballers bestowing awards on sports writers. That'll be the day!

For over eight years I have had the responsibility of the chairmanship of the PFA. For thirteen years I have shared responsibility on the PFA committee. There comes a time in any person's career when responsibility, if accepted, can have a maturing effect and a stabilising influence. I once asked George Best if he would be interested in serving on the PFA committee. The invitation took him by surprise: 'Yes,' he said. 'Very interested.' The intention was, so I thought at the time, for him to take over from Bobby Charlton, who was getting near the end of his playing career with Manchester United. I suppose it's ironical, when you consider Best's antipathy towards his old United colleague and the way he has criticised him in Michael Parkinson's biography, *Best*. But the PFA was involved in important negotiations and needed the game's 'big guns' up front. George would have been a useful committee member. Shortly after the suggestion had been put to him, his troubles began building towards a climax and his subsequent departure from the game in England.

If he had joined the PFA committee it is possible that his career might have been saved. He could have extended his range through new responsibilities. He would have been encouraged to take himself more seriously and would have been taken more seriously by others.

There is more to the game than playing it for ninety minutes on Saturday afternoons. George could have done a great deal for the game and for himself if the timing had been right with a vacancy on the PFA committee before events moved against him at Old Trafford, through his own wilfulness.

His waywardness in what should have been his heyday deprived British football of the greatest footballing talent I have known, but it is gratifying to find that he has at last acknowledged the errors of his ways and while there is time left for him, he has returned to British soccer, at Hibs. His fantastic drawing power was demonstrated when he played in Bobby Robson's testimonial, before joining Hibs, and boosting the Ipswich manager's fund to a reputed £40,000. He could still 'turn it on' even though he had not played for six months. Hibs were reported to be paying him £2000 a game, but that is an investment, easily recoverable from the increased attendances his presence attracts. I am pleased his genius has come in from the cold of American soccer, where he was really only an exhibition player.

Talking of talent being lost, Rodney Marsh might also have made better and longer progress in the English League if he had learned to control his impatience. His independent turn of mind was admirable in many ways. He was a creative player and could talk as well as he played, but he talked himself out of the game and the last I heard he was with Tampa Bay Rowdies. I hate to see players like this going out of the English League. They may enjoy a better lifestyle in American football, but I doubt if they get the same satisfaction that comes from playing at top level in the English League, which is still the best and the most competitive in the world.

Ten

If I had not joined the PFA committee I would probably have gone out of the game as I came into it, with blinkers. Dealing with the game's history and trying to find a common ground in matter involving conditions of employment widened my perspectives.

The hierarchy, of course, includes the Managers' and Secretaries' Association. I have been often asked if I would like to be a manager and join that august company. Each time I have replied that I would not want to be associated with the present managerial system, but no one has asked why I wouldn't. The reason is that I could not adapt to a system which emanates from soccer's feudal structure. Managers are professionals at the mercy of directors, who are amateurs. It seems to me palpably absurd that men who are supposed to know the game inside-out and be devoted to it should be hired and fired by boards of directors whose real business might range from housebuilding to pork butchering. The football ignorance of many directors is legendary. All players have their favourite stories to illustrate what the average director knows about the game, which one eminent player summed up in his autobiography in a blank page. One of my favourite stories – fact not fiction – concerns a director at Leicester who suggested to the manager a sure-fire way of scoring goals from corners. His plan was for Davy Gibson to jump on Mike Stringfellow's back when a corner was coming over and head the ball in! No goalkeeper, he reasoned, could outleap a player on another player's back. The plan was not put into practice. Another suggestion was to train with a rugger ball. The director who had this brainwave pointed out that if we could control an oval ball we would have no trouble controlling a round one.

It is easy to be cynical about directors and ridicule their involvement in the game. There are plenty whose main interest

134

is social and who enjoy the power and prestige a directorship brings. They get a kick out of dispensing the gins-and-tonic to local VIP's in the boardrooms and like to be seen arriving in their Jags, Jensens, Bentleys or Rolls-Royces on the club car park. But there are just as many directors passionately involved in the game, craving success just as much as supporters.

It makes no difference to me whether their interest is sporting or social. It is the system itself which I resent, a system rooted in the past and ultimately destructive. Friction is bound to occur. Boardroom squabbles and rifts are inevitable when there are directors of conflicting views on the same board – classic examples being Derby County and Aston Villa.

A manager may be given freedom of action and full authority, but to some extent he is bound to remain an underling, even a lackey. He has to keep his board of directors happy. Directors want success. They don't know how to achieve it, so they put their faith in a manager whose job is to choose the players and the team to achieve success. His job is to keep the players happy and make sure they are as fit as possible, while devising a playing policy that will satisfy supporters.

Put like that it sounds simple. Theoretically, it is simple. In practice, it is extremely difficult, as the fall out rate among managers testifies. Since the war 1000 managers have bitten the dust. Obviously many of them were not managerial material in the first place and were wrongly chosen by directors whose judgment was at fault.

Sometimes they cannot separate the wheat from the chaff and get into a muddle when they try. There was a manager, hired on a five-year contract and made redundant within twelve months. The matter was settled out of court. The directors then appointed another manager, whom they later sacked. So it goes on, the giddy not-so-merry-go-round, creaking under the rusty mechanism which keeps it going.

If a manager feels his directors have a down on him, he may transfer the burden on to his players. 'What's wrong with the boss today?' 'Oh, just one of his moods.' 'Why does he take it out on us?' 'Who else has he got to take it out of?'

In eighteen years I have served under more bad than good managers, more incompetent than competent ones. I have been

135

bewildered and amused by the set-ups and am still trying to sort out the difference between a general manager and a team manager, a coach and a trainer. I have seen assistant managers who have managed managers and have wondered if a general manager manages the team manager or if he just manages nothing in particular.

In spite of a general opinion among managers who have not been kindly disposed towards me, I have never wanted to manage any of the clubs for which I have played, even when the upheavals taking place stirred me to make known my opinions. At Peterborough, for instance, there was a rift between the directors and the supporters' club. The supporters had raised a lot of money and naturally they wanted to be sure it was put to good use. This created a suspicion among the directors that the supporters' club was interfering in matters which did not concern it.

I saw what was going on and felt there were a few heads that might have benefited from being banged together. A little common sense and mutual confidence could have healed the rift, but it only widened. I spoke to the manager, Gordon Clark, who listened sympathetically, as he always did, being that sort of man. But there was nothing I could do because I was only a player and players, under the system which gives them no authority or autonomy in a club, are supposed to mind their own business, which is confined to the pitch. If players had been allowed to express their views and their views had been acted on, the clubs I left in frustration would probably have avoided the shambles that befell them.

Living under constant pressure from boards of directors, whose attitudes can be determined by whims, power shuffles, boardroom manœuvres and changes of mood, it is surprising more managers don't have nervous breakdowns. I wouldn't want to be a party to such systems. And yet I know I am manager material. How then to stay in the game and at the same time avoid the odds stacked against a manager? The jobs open to a player in the game when his playing career ends are few – manager, assistant manager, coach, trainer.

In the early days of my career I was branded a trouble-maker. Now I am seen by the game's Establishment as a 'leper'. I was regarded as a trouble-maker by those in the game who believed that a player should keep his mouth closed, speak non-controversially when he was spoken to and never step out of line. This was not my way. I believed in speaking up for myself and later, when I became chairman of the PFA, I saw it was my duty to speak up for players, whose rights have been denied by the game's administration for over seventy years.

I knew that I was making myself unpopular among club chairmen, directors and managers when the PFA pressed ahead with freedom of contract proposals. They would have preferred the status quo to have remained unchallenged. Although there was plenty of evidence to show how this was ruining the game, on and off the pitch, they seemed to be locked in a Victorian fantasy world, where authority justified itself and radical proposals could be dismissed as impertinent and irrelevant eccentricities.

When they saw that the PFA 'meant business' and was determined to put footballers on a par with other industries, they agreed to negotiate. The wind of change was gathering force and they had to trim their sails. So did the PFA.

Over three years of negotiation we made various concessions and eventually towards the end of the 1977–8 season, the league chairmen accepted a qualified form of freedom of contract, but failed to accept a system by which a club would be compensated with a multiplying factor which included a player's age, divisional status and experience when he moved on. And I predict they'll live to regret not implementing the multiplying formula devised by the PFA in the long term interest of the game.

In this respect, six Midlands clubs – Coventry, Birmingham, Wolves, Stoke, West Bromwich and Aston Villa – were stubborn and seemed determined to impede all the progress made over three years. I called them 'six mavericks' and the PFA warned that they risked legal proceedings if players could only get their rights by recourse to the law.

What other trade or profession would have been so patient. Footballers are much maligned. They are accused of being quick tempered, provocative, at times aggressive and self-interested. And yet in negotiations between their union and the Football League management committee, they have insisted on patient negotiation when their counterparts in other industries would have resorted to strike action. We have never had a players' strike. The history of the PFA has been peaceful, but this is not to say that the union has been complacent. Far from it. The PFA has been mindful of its members' interests and at the same time the interests of those who maintain the national supporters on the terraces and in the stands.

We could have gone to court to press our claims, satisfied that we would have had the force of law behind us. 'Restraint of trade' is frowned on by the courts, as the Kerry Packer case has proved. What is the registration retention system as applied by clubs, when players' contracts have expired, if not restraint of trade?

During negotiations our respect for the league's management committee grew. They realised that these changes had to come, that the modern footballer differs from his predecessors in that he will not accept serfdom and expects to be treated as an equal in a profession which depends entirely on his skill, dedication and sense of responsibility.

My determination has been to get a fair deal for players. I could have thumped the table and made demands. But, where would this have got us? Nowhere. A gap would have opened between players and the authorities. It would have been 'them' and 'us'. We are all in the game together and by compromising (on detail, not our principles) we demonstrated our willingness to work out a package deal acceptable to both sides.

Until I chaired regional meetings of footballers, to explain the freedom of contract proposals, I did not know the meaning of power. At seven regional meetings I was in a powerful position, as chairman of the PFA, to influence members at the start of the 1977–8 season. But it was opportunity, not power, that appealed to me; the opportunity to explain to members exactly what the PFA sought and why we regarded the proposals as the most important in our association's history. It would have been possible to present the plan as a fait accompli and to ask members to underwrite it. This was never our intention. No player was asked to vote for something which had been decided for him, nor to give his support to something he did not adequately understand.

I welcomed the opportunity to meet members and, with Cliff

138

Lloyd, and George Davies, our solicitor, to spell out the pros and cons of the proposals.

All the implications were set before the players in a straight-forward manner. There was no attempt to 'lead' them, nor to ask them to rubber-stamp something they did not understand. I was aware of being in a position denied to football managers. Whereas they deal with perhaps a few dozen players, I was dealing with the best part of 2500. Only a handful opposed the proposals and it is significant that they were from a few of the Midland clubs whose hierarchies banded together to try to thwart the proposals.

I noticed a couple of players from West Bromwich, a couple from Stoke and a couple from Coventry City, who were them-selves in privileged positions, emerge as antagonists. These were players who did not have to worry about anything, because they were doing more than all right in the game, which gave them their living. I had the impression that they had allowed them-selves to be gently intimidated by their clubs and were reflect-ing the official views of their employers. One might say they were 'playing safe'. Their less privileged colleagues, however, did not go along with them.

The West Midlands meeting lasted longer than meetings in any other part of the country, nearly four hours. As chairman of the PFA before putting the issue to a vote, which was to give the PFA management committee power to press for our pro-posals to be implemented, by industrial action if necessary, I ensured that everyone attending a meeting knew precisely what was involved. I would always say: 'If there is anyone with a point to raise or it is not absolutely certain what the issues are, please speak up.' I was aware that in small groups, foot-ballers are usually more confident than in a large hall, sur-rounded by scores or hundreds of fellow members. I wanted to be sure that no one was too shy or diffident to get to his feet and speak his mind.

If anyone was against the proposals, I welcomed his inter-vention. There was no rancour or malice. As the PFA's chair-man it was not for me to pronounce something which did not have the complete support of members. My only reason for staying on was to see through the proposals which the PFA began negotiating in January 1975. It irked me to hear various

139

managers and directors claim that once the proposals had been implemented, I would be 'scarpering' and leaving others to get on with the new system. By the same token they could accuse me of enjoying power for its own sake and taking advantage of the proposals merely to stay on as chairman.

I am not that cynical. It would have been impractical to get the negotiations underway and then resign as chairman to pass on the complicated issues to another chairman. I was interested only in continuity, which meant remaining until negotiations had been completed and the new deal implemented. It was not the full PFA committee which was responsible for the negotiations; only a sub-committee of three, the chairman of the PFA; the president of the Football League; two members of the management committee of both organisations and the respective secretaries.

I was annoyed when Jimmy hill, a former chairman of the PFA and now managing director of Coventry City, took issue with the proposals and opposed the multiplying factor that had been worked out and approved by the League management committee. This was a heavy spanner thrown into delicate works. It was hard for me to reconcile his attitude with his pronouncements when he was chairman of the PFA.

In 1961 he published a book, *Striking for Soccer* (Peter Davies), in which he argued the case for a player having the freedom to move from his club. A player, he said, 'should be able to move merely because he wants to.' He was firmly against the retain-and-transfer system.

It would be reassuring to believe that everyone in the game has a secure future, but that would be wishful thinking. It is still a profession of terrible insecurity, even at the highest level. I often wonder if those who 'sell' the game, the likes of the former PFA chairman Jimmy Hill, are as secure as they appear. As a player, Jimmy Hill was less than distinguished. In his 269 appearances for Fulham, he scored only forty goals, and in his 83 League games for Brentford, scored only ten goals. That is a total of fifty goals in 352 appearances. I will say this for him – that since he finished playing, he has become a better player! Now and again he tells us on television of 'the five' he scored at Doncaster. Were they goals or mounts?

Jimmy Hill had the best opportunity of his career in working

140

with Cliff Lloyd (in my view the finest administrator the game has produced) and with solicitor George Davies. The PFA's administration was strong and Jimmy Hill had only to 'front' it while the hard work in getting the maximum wage abolished during his term of office, was done behind the scenes. During his four years as chairman he got a great deal of publicity and became a public figurehead, but none of this would have come his way without the conscientious work of Cliff Lloyd and George Davies.

Having read his book recently, I wonder if he feels any embarrassment about what appears to me a turn-about, which is why I have accused him of being 'a poacher turned game-keeper'. The way in which he and his associates at the six maverick clubs who opposed the qualified form of freedom of contract, contradicts the ideals he represented when he was chairman of the PFA.

I am against anyone who tries to hinder and hamper the PFA from getting rightful conditions for its members. Jimmy Hill has done well out of the game. He enjoys a comfortable lifestyle and on Match of the Day he is regarded as the game's national sage. I wish he had retained and not turned his back on the sympathies and principles he embodied as PFA chairman, between 1957–61.

In ten years' time I hope I shall be able to look back on what the PFA has achieved and be proud of the part I played in the changes. We have had to overcome tyranny, coercion and blatant unfairness, which for too long have been meekly tolerated in the profession. All players, from apprentices and schoolboys to contract players, young and old, are now guaranteed a New Deal and with it the respect that should be paid to them as human beings, under the proposals patiently and painstakingly worked out over three and a half years.

I shall never be in the position of Jimmy Hill, who has gone back on the words and sentiments expressed in his auto-biography. If his autobiography had been ghost-written, I could have made some allowance and said, well, the words were not his own. He could have been misrepresented. But he assured us, from the start, that he had not engaged a ghost-writer and the book was his and his alone. What he wrote in 1961 he appeared in the mid-seventies to have contradicted.

141

The documentation he used at the time in his book came from Cliff Lloyd. He drew on the facts and experience compiled by the PFA to present a case which as a public personality on TV and as managing director of Coventry City, he later opposed.

I like to think that in later years I shall not be against change because of some current vested interest. What I have written, here, will remain true ten years from now.

And the truth is that footballers, if they say their prayers, should give thanks to Cliff Lloyd himself a former professional footballer, for his tireless efforts on their behalf. I too am grateful to him. On 29 August 1957 when I arrived in the English League after four years with Distillery, I little imagined that I would eventually become chairman of the PFA. Nor did I anticipate a phone call I would receive when I was with Leicester City:

'Hello, Derek, I'm Cliff Lloyd secretary of the PFA ...' What, I wondered had I done. Had I transgressed and was about to be taken to task by my union. I said: 'What can I do for you?' Cliff invited me to join the union's committee. When I accepted the invitation, I was adding a new dimension to my career.

At the time I did not realise that my acceptance would be interpreted by some managers and directors as a determination to set myself against them, that all I was interested in was upsetting that status quo and challenging their authority. They could not or would not see that the PFA was interested only in serving the game itself and improving conditions not only for members but for everyone who cares for the game. There are no divided loyalties, as far as the PFA is concerned. The benefits obtained for members, help to benefit the game and so benefit all who follow the game.

To their credit, some managements and clubs accepted the new changes were inevitable. They understood that the PFA was not interested in change for its own sake, but for the good of the game. While some managers and boards treated me as a leper, others appreciated that I was only trying to get a better deal for players in an industry traditionally hidebound and autocratic. Once they realised that I was not a table-thumper, who demands instead of proposing, they responded and listened attentively to the proposals.

A revolution has occurred. But it has been achieved by evolutionary means, not by industrial action and confrontation. If Cliff Lloyd and I had been revolutionary radicals, we would have exerted pressure on the industry and called footballers out on strike. This would have disrupted the game and driven away supporters on whom the game depends. At every stage of negotiations we had the good of the game at heart and showed that the PFA is not a militant movement, but a progressive organisation which values the interests of all that the profession represents.

Changes were long overdue. They could not have been achieved overnight or in a season. The PFA had to overcome a prejudice that the changes would only benefit the rich clubs. The same argument was used to oppose the abolition of the maximum wage. 'We were told the rich club would get richer and the poor, poorer.' Nineteen years later we knew this was a fallacy.

We set out to prove that if radical changes were not made, fewer clubs would be in a position to look at the future with any degree of security. A handful of prosperous clubs controlled the transfer market and made the money. The prevailing system was not equitable; nor did it respect the players' professionalism.

In future, footballers will have greater opportunities to direct the course of their careers and inept managers will have fewer opportunities to impose their waywardness on the profession.

The present system favours bad management. The new deal favours initiative, enterprise and freedom of movement, in line with such surveys as the 1968 Chester Report and CIR report to which the PFA contributed evidence and made recommendations.

Football is a flowing, changing game; above all, its essence is spontaneity. When it is controlled by preconceived notions and set patterns, it stultifies, on and off the pitch. Change must come, at all levels of the game. Players are not automatons to be set in motion for ninety minutes on Saturday afternoons. They live the game all the time, which is why the PFA has been mindful of the conditions in which they operate. A discontented, frustrated player is not likely to make the best use of his talent. A player who feels that he is being unfairly treated

143

will either withdraw from the game or fail to fulfil his full potential. He will become disenchanted and lose interest.

Everyone knows of past players who ended on the scrapheap. But for the PFA, this would still be true. The appointment of a full-time education officer, to advise and guide young players in their future careers, after they have finished playing, guarantees that no player should finish on Skid Row, if he takes advantage of all the services and advice now offered by his association.

There is a world of difference between playing the game and making a living away from football. The PFA has tried to bridge the gap, facilitating the transition. This was unknown to a previous generation of footballers. So too was freedom of contract.

In a foreword to Jimmy Guthrie's autobiography, *Soccer Rebel* (Pentagon, 1976), Danny Blanchflower alleged that the PFA had done as much for Jimmy Hill and myself as we have done for the union. He explained that it had given us a public platform to become more conspicuous than we might have been without it. 'They worked for the cause in its day of limelight when any sort of union noise was food for the media. The cause helped Jimmy Hill and Dougan become TV personalities.'

Such cynicism is beneath contempt. It is some years since I was a 'TV personality', and that was only through my involvement in a World Cup panel. My chairmanship of the PFA has not brought, or sought any TV personality lustre. One might argue that Danny Blanchflower's captaincy of Tottenham Hotspur gave him the limelight of a Sunday newspaper sports column. In what seems to be a cynical age, I do not expect such cynics as Danny Blanchflower to believe that my only reason for remaining as chairman of the PFA was to carry through to their conclusion proposals initiated during my chairmanship. I appreciate what Jimmy Guthrie has done for the association, but Danny's remarks in the foreword of this book, made me smile. For the record, when negotiations began I had been on the PFA committee for nearly ten years and five years as chairman.

Glory-seeking is more conspicuous off the pitch, than in tiring complicated negotiations with the football authorities. Having completed negotiations, I am now looking ahead – to who knows what? People ask me what the future holds. I can only repeat Mort Sahl's immortal phrase, that the future lies ahead.

When I was a raw recruit to league football, I soon discovered that no one was going to help and advise me. At my first three clubs in the English League, I looked in vain for senior professionals to pass on the fruits of their experience, to warn me of the pitfalls and advise me what to expect in the profession. Not one offered a word of advice or even encouragement. It seemed they were so insecure that their minds were centred on keeping their own places in the sides and they had no time, or thought, for a newcomer. It was not until I plunged from Aston Villa in the first division to Peterborough, in the third, that I evaluated my career and realised that if I did not make special efforts I risked hurtling down Skid Row. As it turned out, I had eleven years to go in first class football, but I would have been lucky to survive another eleven months if I had not pulled myself together.

Few people succeed by their own efforts. In my years as a professional footballer, I came to appreciate the standards set by a number of people who stimulated and inspired me – in no order of merit, my wife, Jutta; Cliff Lloyd, George Davies, Alan Lambert, Dr Percy Young (he wrote *The History of Wolverhampton Wanderers* and *The History of British Football*), Ray Seaton, a journalist; Mr George Watts and Mr Roy Pearson, who finally cured my back trouble. They have been interrelated in my career and have helped me to formulate a working philosophy which has governed my approach to the game, on and off the pitch.

Football is more than a game; it is a way of life. That is why the PFA has pressed so vigorously for players to be treated with the respect they deserve as members of a democratic community. Their way of life, for generations, has been one of bondage and a denial of their ordinary rights. In spite of what the autocrats who administer the game, like to pretend to preserve their own authority, footballers do care about their freedom, which is the freedom of the individual in whatever trade or profession he makes his living. If all players had the lifestyle of Kevin Keegan, Trevor Francis and Tony Woodcock, there would be no need for the PFA. Few players are within nodding distance of the good fortune which has come their way.

They rely on the PFA to represent their interests and try to improve their conditions, and look after their welfare.

To a certain extent, the profession has won a sort of freedom.

It is foolish and misleading of Danny Blanchflower to compare me with Jimmy Hill. As chairman of the PFA I was involved in far more crucial issues. My active involvement has not been surpassed by any other player this century, with the exception of Cliff Lloyd, OBE.

If Danny Blanchflower and his ilk had done their bit, as I did, my predecessors would have had a better deal.

I struggled for achievement on and off the pitch, not just for personal glory which any player covets, but for the good of my profession and the satisfaction that comes with striving for worthwhile targets. On the pitch, I felt pride in being the only Irishman to score more than 200 English League goals, surpassing the record set by the immortal Peter Doherty, a former Irish international. I also did something no Wolves player of old managed to do, score nine goals in European competition in one season, thus joining the good company of Dennis Viollet and Denis Law. No Spurs player, even in Danny Blanchflower's time, did this. Only Stan Bowles has gone one better.

As a makeshift centre forward, I lasted nearly twenty years in the first division, with over 600 appearances.

My 'longevity' as chairman of the PFA was not to test my staying power, but to see through the complicated freedom of contract proposals.

At present they are a diluted version of what footballers have every right to expect and I am sure, will eventually get. After so many years of intransigence by the football authorities, what has been gained is a big improvement on the conditions which previous generations of footballers accepted with hardly a murmur of resentment. We are at last on the right road, but there is still some distance to travel before the PFA, on behalf of its members, is satisfied. I didn't just buck against the system; I was determined to change it, on behalf of players throughout the league.

Clubs have been warned. The red light is not yet shining, but the amber light is on and they are in no doubt that the PFA is prepared to press its legitimate claims. They have been told in no uncertain terms, in a letter to the Football League,

23 March 1978, that the association deserves the right to take whatever action it considers necessary to remove any restrictions on members. We are not prepared to deviate from our principles. For the first time – and not before time – players after completing their contracts have a say in deciding which clubs they play for – a democratic right denied to them for generations.

For me, football is a way of life, which I have continued to live after my retirement from the playing side of it. And I shall go on living the game, until the final whistle.

Endpiece

Ten years ago, in my first book, *Attack!*, I predicted that the next generation would produce millionaire footballers. At the time, my prediction was scorned as exaggerated fancy, mere wishful thinking. And yet it has come to pass.

My estimation was based on the recognition that it is not managers, coaches, chairman and directors, administrators and legislators, the crowds flock to see, but the players. It is the players the Press and TV crews want to film and to interview, because the players *are* the game. There is no game without them.

In previous generations they were treated as serfs and paid slave wages. Even established stars, idols of the stands and terraces, were not much better off than the ordinary, uncelebrated player and once they had reached the end of their playing days, they could be dumped on the scrapheap.

Attitudes and values have changed and are continuing to change, for the better. But there is still a long way to go. Some die-hard attitudes still exist among legislators, whose minds remain implanted in the nineteenth century. A man can make a mistake once and be forgiven; if he repeats the mistake, he is a fool. If he makes the same mistake a third time, he is an incompetent fool. So be it for many of todays legislators.

I have tried in this book to show the sort of obstacles, hurdles and hazards a player may encounter and the resentment an independent-minded player might meet when he tries to assert his views for the good of his profession. In spite of the game's ingrained conservatism and reluctance to change, radical improvements are taking place.

Within the next five years, perhaps sooner, I predict that footballers will have full freedom of contract, so that when they have fulfilled the conditions of their contracts, their clubs will not be compensated for their departure. They will be able to move on, like people in any other profession.

I hope and believe that before long they will enjoy the rights, liberties and self-determination to which they are entitled. Their only demand is to be treated with respect.

* * *

* * *